I Changed My Mind ...
It Changed My Life

THE STORY OF A SABOTEUR, A MUSE
AND THE WOMAN IN-BETWEEN

DARLA CLAIRE, CHt

What people are saying...

"Many of us face 'experiences' in our formative years that we carry with us for the rest of our lives. It could be something traumatic or sad or something that brings us great joy. But how we 'nurture' and carry those experiences forward can impact everything that we do and how we engage with others. Darla talks about her inner struggles based on her experiences in her childhood and the evolution from someone who forced 'her muse' to be overshadowed by her 'saboteur' self. We all do this to one extent or another in life, and many find it hard to search inward to understand the origins of the struggle. Darla brings a genuine, vivid, and open elucidation of how she charted her path toward both inner and outer healing.

This very touching story of her saboteur who interacts, through her coping mechanisms and artistic strength, demonstrates that to find your inner muse you must openly chart your journey. She demonstrates, through her experiences, how everyone's journey is based on their own fears and strengths that they bring to the healing process. Finally, Darla writes with true empathy and understanding of how this is not an easy process but coming out the other side is a wonderful reward that we all deserve."

~ Ingrid M. Martin, Ph.D, Director of Graduate Programs
Professor of Marketing, College of Business Administration, CSU

"A beautiful, inspiring and touching story of how a woman emerges from a life that felt not fully lived into one with deep self-understanding, greater peace and joy. As the author grapples with internal conflict, she uncovers parts of herself that she disliked, parts that created chaos and pain, and that she wanted to dismiss and disregard. She intuited that if you dismiss any part of yourself, it is the same as negating the whole self, which then sustains low self-esteem, maintains self-dislike, and continues the splintering of self. From her deep commitment to evolve into a healthier being, she recognized she ultimately needed to get to know, befriend, find compassion, and even love these parts in order to become more whole and heal her life.

From this process and addressing these universal themes, the author developed a brilliant and powerful process that would be important for all of us to learn and put into practice. This story is told in an easy-to-read, friendly, creative and approachable style, and I fully recommend it."

~ Taffy Clarke Pelton, MA, LPC Psychotherapist,
Life Coach, Author

"Darla Claire gracefully demonstrates how you can change your mind and change your life. She shares her journey of taming her inner critic to reclaim her personal power and inspires us to do the same. When you are ready for your inner critic to become the champion of your dreams, I highly recommend reading this book and applying the steps to your life."

~ Lisa Manyon
The Business Marketing Architect and President of
Write On Creative.

"Darla Claire's memoir chronicles her struggle with her internal Saboteur. Her personal story expresses a common theme that many people struggle with at some point during their life, which is a battle with a harsh, self-sabotaging inner critic. Darla's dedication to exploring her inner 'demons' enabled her to evolve from a tormented inner life into a woman whose life is now filled with peace and joy. I admire Darla for her vulnerability and her willingness to open her heart and share her story. I also believe Darla's story will be an inspiration to other people who struggle with their own personal internal Saboteur."

~ Dr. Ross Pelton, The Natural Pharmacist, Author

"This is a beautiful book which addresses the inner saboteur. Author Darla Claire shares her journey of how she discovered her inner saboteur, made peace with her, replaced the critic that was holding her back and leveraged her saboteur's strengths to achieving her life goals. In I Changed My Mind ... It Changed My Life, she inspires and encourages us all to identify our inner saboteur by sharing the tools that she used so that we can do the same. I highly recommend this book. It changed my mind and has elevated my life."

~ Joie Gharrity – Founder 113 Branding

"Darla Claire is more than a writer she is a brilliant storyteller! She shares her story by taking us along on her personal journey, weaving words, clearly explaining, and cleverly introducing us to the inner critic, the Saboteur and Divine spirit ... the Muse. This is a unique, fresh and powerful take on how to stop fighting 'ourselves' and start living peacefully with those often, un-acknowledged parts of our inner being. A clarifying read!"

~ Joyce Klaver, Certified NLP Life Coach, Master Hypnotist

Dedication

To Meridian Kristi, my beloved friend: I am forever grateful for our precious creative girl time together in Florida.

To the fabulous women of the Rogue Moxies in southern Oregon: You are my beloved tribe and I am inspired by the friendships that have grown into an amazing sisterhood.

To my husband, Michael, my true love, best friend and #1 fan. Thank you for being you.

To my first love,

Dad

love you more ...

xo

Contents

Introduction
MY LETTER TO YOU

I made a promise to myself in December of 2018 that I would do two things. One, was to write this book and two, was to create art on a regular basis. My number one goal was to write this book for myself; it was a challenge I wanted to complete. I was also writing this for my daughter ... leaving her a part of me she may not know through this book as part of my legacy.

When I was writing this story, I realized it was bigger than just my daughter and me. I was writing it for you.

You are also my BIG WHY.

I used to believe I couldn't follow my dreams, I couldn't manifest my desires into reality, and I couldn't be free. I saw just about everyone else as being brave, more successful AND doing what they loved. I believed I wasn't good enough, wasn't smart enough, didn't have enough education, wasn't young enough, wealthy enough and certainly not brave enough.

I was afraid ...

I was afraid but that was because I had learned to believe my thoughts as truth. I wanted to be an artist; I wanted to be successful in my pursuits; I wanted a relationship that was reliable, good and full of love. I wanted to be brave enough to spread my wings and fly!

I didn't believe I could have any of it. I'd actually given up on most of what I wanted in life. Maybe I was too hard on myself, but on the other hand I had learned to believe my thoughts as truth. Little did I know, this couldn't have been any farther from the truth.

In the middle of what I referred to as "living in the in-between," I became comfortable living my uncomfortable life. I was jolted awake by what I can only describe as an intervention from my Divine Source. I was shaken up by Source and facing my fear of dealing with my internal Saboteur that was filled with dialogue of lies and untruths about myself.

Until then, I believed those thoughts to be true, or at the least, I let them form my opinion of myself ... which wasn't a very good one.

This is the story about the time I heard loud and clear from Source and what to do about my lifelong self-sabotage.

I share my circumstances and emotions that were keeping me in a life of mediocrity. I'm not an unusual woman; I'm probably much like you, and you're like me in many ways. I believe that you'll see a bit of yourself in my personal journey of self-discovery. You most likely have common threads of emotions. Those types of emotions have stopped me in my tracks more times than I care to remember.

If the sacred download hadn't taken place, I wouldn't have been changed in such a profound way. I no longer live in the in-between. I am living my dream life and following my Joy every day!

I will never go back.

I share the events that led up to the day I received what I call the "sacred download" and how my life unfolded in the following weeks and years. I was given step by step instructions to help save myself from continuing a life of mediocrity. Seeing my Saboteur for the first time I felt a rush of emotions of anger and sadness. As she became fully revealed I found I had very different feelings and a new perspective. The old saying that "knowledge is power" is so true when it comes to intimately learning about yourself, which gave me a power that I'd never had before.

I introduce you to my spirit guide. I call her the Muse. Meeting her is the first time I actually felt a sense of purpose that had substance I could sink my teeth into. I have a clear picture of purpose that has since become my mantra ... all with gratitude for intimately learning to know my Muse, my joy seeker.

I thought there were two parts of the download, however the word "weave" kept coming into my head. I then realized that I am as much of a part of the equation as the other two parts. Knowing this, everything building up to this point made sense to me and it all fell together.

It was a powerful day in my life.

As you continue to read the following pages, may it enlighten you, strengthen you and change your mind, which can in turn can change your life. It changed my life in a fabulous way and through sharing, it has changed many others lives as well ...

In Peace and Love,

YOUR LIFESTYLE ARCHITECT

1

The Root Cause

We often don't remember the unremarkable days of our childhood, instead we simply remember those significantly bad or good ones.

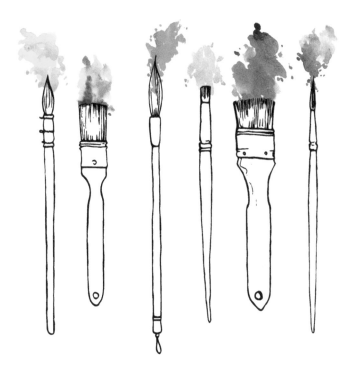

I'd never been so humiliated in my life!

The first thing I think of when thinking about my primary school days, is an incident involving a teacher I looked up to, admired and respected. I remember being in the 5th grade and was about 10 years old. My teacher, Mr. Bailey had assigned us to read a book, write a report and then be prepared to present to the class. I'd finished my assignment on time, felt confident in the homework I'd done, and was happy to give the report to the class. I raised my hand volunteering to go first.

Mr. Bailey was the youngest teacher I'd had and probably the youngest teacher at the elementary school. He was my first male teacher, not that it matters. I remember thinking he was kind of cute, even with his big horned-rimmed glasses covering most of his face. I had a secret crush on him.

When it was time for me to get up in front of the class, I don't remember being nervous or anxious at all. I had lots of friends. I made sure I was wearing a cute new dress my mom had made and I confidently walked to the front of the room to present my book report. As I was finishing up, I was feeling proud of myself. It went seamlessly and it felt like a big accomplishment for my first big kid speech. I was sure I was going to get an A. I neatly folded the notes I'd written and waited for Mr. Bailey to comment before heading back to my desk in the middle of the classroom.

My teacher got up from his chair at the front of the room, looked at me, and said I did a good job. He then asked me to turn around. Being the "good girl," I obeyed him and turned around with my back to my classmates. Immediately, the entire class burst out into laughter, including Mr. Bailey. I was horrified. The teacher had me turn around because I was standing a little too close to the blackboard at the front of the class and I had chalk all over the backside of my new dress. Mr. Bailey obviously thought he was being funny and perhaps wanted to let the other students know what not to do when it was their turn. I could feel the heat rushing to my face. There was no hiding my embarrassment. I could only hear a loud roar in my head. I felt myself swirling and getting dizzy as I made my way back to my desk. I literally wanted to crawl into a hole and die. I wanted to run away and never ever face my classmates again. The crush I'd been carrying for the young cute teacher abruptly ended.

That incident was one of those significant incidents that literally became a part of me, and not in a good way. Prior to Mr. Bailey's humiliation of me, I was confident in school, was friends with all of my classmates and had no hesitation to volunteer for tasks in front of the class or for the whole school for that matter.

I believe we are all born with a clean slate with our main mode of operation as a pure subconscious being. As pure creative beings, we are perfect, with no ideas that we are limited or not good enough in any manner. Yet, as soon as our mental capacity is in the emotional development stage, the opportunity for forming opinions of ourselves and our abilities (or inabilities in some cases) becomes part of our psyche. Generally, the most impactful time for attaching self-esteem to ourselves is when we're in the formative childhood years.

GROWING UP ...

I was born into a middle-class family, with a Dad, a stay-at-home Mother, an older brother, a herding dog named "Bo" and my orange tabby cat "Tiger." I assumed we were a typical middle-class family living in Southern California. We always had food on our table, wore nice clothes and lived in a clean, well actually, spotless house. My parents owned their home and my mom's parents lived next door. Our family vacations were few and on a tight budget, but I had no idea we weren't wealthy. My dad always made things fun and mom had a creative knack for making our home look beautiful. Close to where we lived, we'd go horseback riding on a nearby ranch where my parents raised corn and cattle. We'd go to the beach, build sandcastles, eat ice cream and ride the waves with our bodies.

When I was in the middle of my elementary school years, we moved to Ashland, Oregon. My parents wanted to get out of the rat race of Southern California. In Oregon, we'd spend many of our summers on Shasta Lake camping, as my mom used to say "the clean way" ... on a houseboat that my dad and his friend had built. We water-skied and fished, baked in the sun, sat around the campfire at night roasting marshmallows for the gooey s'mores and consuming way too much sugar. We'd listen to my Dad tell us tales of fun adventures and sometimes scary stories after we'd crawled into bed. Our sleeping bags were laid in a perfectly lined row on the top deck of the houseboat with a ceiling of thousands upon thousands of stars filling the night sky with an occasional satellite speeding across.

I do believe I had a pretty good childhood; normal is what I thought. I spent hours upon hours imagining, taking myself to a different place, a perfect place, where I was a princess, always feeling safe. So it was pretty easy for me to (in my mind) have had the perfect childhood. But that wasn't the whole truth. I became good at pretending and actually believed my own storybook lie. That lie followed me into adulthood and if something contradicted the lie and was painful, I conveniently forgot it. It was just not a part of my story. I surrounded myself with my pretend bubble and from the outside looking in, it all looked pretty perfect. I became an expert in ignoring it, pretending that everything was good by daydreaming that my life was great. It was easy to have people believe me, I just put on my smile and would quietly sing to myself the song my dad taught me,

"Zip-a-dee-doo-dah ... Zip-a-dee-Ay ... my oh my ... what a wonderful day ... plenty of sunshine heading my way, Zip-a-dee-doo-dah ... Zip-a-dee-Ay!

Mr. Blue Bird on my shoulder, it's the truth, it's actual ... everything is satisfactual ... Zip-a-dee-doo-dah ... Zip-a-dee-Ay ... wonderful feelings wonderful day!"

I don't know why, but I was afraid to expose anything negative about myself or my family in any way to anyone. Like many people who are mistreated, they can feel it's their fault. I was no different; I felt it was my fault. I was embarrassed, afraid and often felt less than, and not good enough.

My mother wasn't a very warm mom. There were no hugs growing up; no tucking me into bed, no bedtime stories, or even telling me she loved me. She did make me beautiful clothes. She was very creative and an exceptional seamstress. When I had a special event or if it was "picture day" in school, I'd wake up to find a pretty new dress she'd made the night before. I'm sure it was her way of showing me she loved me. I believe she'd mostly shut herself off from her intimate feelings. Her self-image was low, although I believe most people didn't know it.

When I was an adult, my mother went through radical breast cancer. My mother shared with me, for the first time, that she felt like she was never good enough, and not wanted from her birth parents because she was adopted. She was devastated when my father asked her for a divorce, and no longer wanted by the only man she truly loved. So this didn't surprise me that she'd passed that gene on to me when I was growing up. As a child she'd tell me I wasn't good enough, but it wasn't outright, it was indirectly. When I received a good grade in school, a B, she'd tell me she got A's. When I brought home A's she told me she skipped a grade. I felt I could never meet her expectations. When cleaning and doing chores around the house, I'd have to do them over until they'd met her standards. She was a perfectionist and wanted her little girl to reflect her perfection.

I remember a few times coming home from school to find my bedroom a complete disaster. If my room wasn't neat and tidy, as to her expectations of everything being folded nicely, put in the right places and hung up properly, she'd pull out everything from my dresser drawers, closet and items under my bed. It was all piled high on top of the bed. It looked like a bomb had gone off in my room. She told me I needed to get things right. It was a lot of pressure and I knew I could never meet her expectations. So, in my mind, I wasn't good enough. And as a result I didn't appreciate my mom very much.

I'm not completely sure why, but my brother was jealous of me. I know my mother favored him; I'm not sure if it was because he was her first born. I'll never know why. I think my brother may have been jealous because of my relationship with our Dad. I was the pretty little girl with golden skin and platinum curls. I was Daddy's little girl. I have an idea it was about me being skinny (my brother was chunky), and my grades were always better than his. It probably had to do with that I was popular in school, and he wasn't so much.

I have an idea that I was his target. He'd lie to my mom. He would blame me for things he did, trying to get me into trouble, and most of the time she believed him. I felt I was constantly in trouble. Most of the time, I'd start crying which turned into, "Why are you crying? You must be lying!"

Behind my mom's back he would hold me down, punch me in the stomach or twist my arms and then act like he did nothing wrong. I'd get the "look" from him that I'd better not tell, or he'd hit me or tell my mom something else to get me in trouble. He became very good with his lies and was convincing. I learned to admit to things I didn't do in hopes of not getting into so much trouble. As we got older my brother's physical abuse became harder. I don't think he realized how strong he was becoming. I did everything I could to avoid him.

For the most part though, I don't remember many details of my childhood. I do remember crying and holding on to my Dad when he left for work because I didn't want him to leave. He worked out of town several hours away in construction, so he'd be gone for days at a time. When he came home from work, I'd run out to his truck before he could get both feet on the ground. I was so happy and relieved to see him.

Daddy treated me like his princess; he made me feel special and loved. I'd sit on his lap when we watched tv together and we'd practice gymnastics on the family room rug where I balanced on his feet up in the air with my arms spread like a bird flying. I remember him often waking me up early in the morning to take me with him for coffee (I had hot chocolate) with him and his buddies at a nearby cafe. I can't remember my brother ever going with us, maybe because Dad didn't invite him or perhaps, he took my brother at times that I wasn't included. Besides a few enduring and fond memories of my Grandmother who lived next door, my girlfriend Cindy that lived a couple houses down the street and Easter Holiday's at my Aunt Gussie's home, I can't remember very much more of my childhood than that.

After that day of humiliation in front of my class, I became fearful of being in front of the class. However, what was worse was I ended up getting nervous even when talking to more than a few friends at a time. That meant whenever there were more than 3 sets of eyes on me while I was talking, I'd feel the heat rising to my face, my throat getting tight, a heaviness around my chest and I became very self-conscious. Over the years I found I avoided everything that involved me speaking, or even remotely resembled getting attention in front of my peers and people of authority. I carried it into adulthood and into my jobs as well—strategically maneuvering my life around anything that involved my speaking, casually talking, and presenting anything that may have included more than those 3 sets of eyes on me.

I had plenty of evidence over the years that confirmed my perceived inabilities. They stemmed from some family dysfunctions, teachers, abusive relationships, some male coworkers and even peers, which made it so easy for me to attach the negative emotions and limiting beliefs about myself. This happens in one way or another to everyone.

Isn't this life after all?

Yes, it was a stupid and a cruel thing Mr. Bailey did to me in grade school. But what I did was to continue the self-ridicule year after year after year. Believing I just wasn't good enough. Believing I was unable to speak my truth. Some people told me they thought I was "stuck up," or aloof. I think they thought I thought I was "better than others," and nothing could have been farther from the truth.

2

The Oprah Show

AND OPPORTUNITIES

Opportunities unrealized:
These are often directly related to
unhealthy mindset habits...in other
words, unconscious stinking thinking.

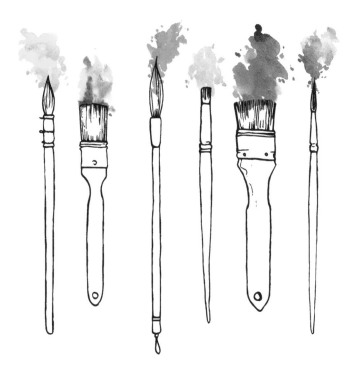

I used to dream of being an artist and clothing designer. I knew I had some talent from the comments I'd receive from family and friends, but most importantly was how I felt when playing around with my art. I could get lost for hours on end drawing, looking through fashion magazines and catalogs, painting, designing clothes ... it was my happy place. Neither of my parents nor my brother were artists at the time, so it was a space just for me.

Heading into High School I picked an art class to take as one of my two electives. I was excited and looking forward to the class. This was going to be my first art lessons and I was eager to get started. Being in high school for the first couple of weeks was pretty intimidating because of the older kids. They'd already learned the ropes of being in High School and they were so much cooler than I was.

I wasn't able to get in the painting class I wanted as it was already full, so instead I signed up for jewelry making. It was a fun class, but I didn't have any of the tools to make them at home. I made a ring and a few pins and necklaces. I did a good job, but my heart wanted to paint. My jewelry teacher told us the painting classes were going to be having an "Art Show" exhibiting their work. I remember the day I went into my art class to find several paintings hung all around the classroom walls and in the windows. They were big paintings, some were framed and looked so professional. I thought they were all beautiful and I was in awe.

However, this was when I decided I couldn't take the art class. The voice in my head told me I wouldn't be good enough, and that I could never paint like these students. This is when I stopped painting and ended my dream of being an artist. I was afraid.

I squelched my dream right then and there because I listened to the part of me that believed I wasn't good enough and I definitely wasn't educated enough. Those thoughts seemed louder than my desire to follow my heart. I was beginning to believe them. And in a way they kept me safe. Safe from failing ... safe from embarrassing myself again.

The limiting beliefs about myself followed me well into adulthood. Even with my successes along the way, my internal negative dialogue and fear were ready at a moment's notice. It had become an automatic physical response before I realized I had any thought. The automatic physical response is when you ((feel)) it in your body before you have a conscious thought about the situation. For example, when I go to the dentist and sit in the "chair," my heart starts to race before I actually have the thought of, "I'm afraid of getting hurt."

After graduating from high school, I moved to Hawaii to spread my wings and see the world. One of my best friends and I went together; she was the bravest girl I knew. To me she was fearless. A few months later, I found out I was in over my head and too afraid to take the perceived risks of being free and on my own! I was still very much a dependent child, so spreading my wings didn't last very long. In looking back at the situation, I can't help but believe the inner voice in my head ended up sabotaging our adventure in paradise.

After several months I found myself back in my hometown and had signed up for sensible business classes at the local university. Within a year I'd gotten married and just a couple months later became pregnant with my beautiful baby girl. We ended up moving to Portland, a much larger city for my husband's work, and it felt like it was an opportunity to again spread my wings in the big city.

As things would have it, we eventually divorced as we were both young and immature, and both made mistakes that were irreparable. I needed to move to another school district for my daughter, as I couldn't afford the private school she'd been attending. We moved to Lake Oswego, a suburb of Portland, and the best school district in the area. Out of financial need and persistence I was able to secure a good job. I was working my way up the ladder as an accounting clerk for a large quasi-state legal firm.

After a few years I ended up holding a top management position, as the Director of Administration. I was overseeing all administration functions and that included reporting directly to the board of directors. The board meetings were held only few times a year, quarterly if my memory serves me well, and yet I found myself using the avoidance tactic. I would conveniently go on vacation, call in sick, or would sign up for a continuing education class. Only a couple of times did I end up reporting to the board in over 12 years of employment with them. When I did give the board members the reports, I had migraines the following two days after each event.

As I watched, some of my coworkers moved on to larger firms, received higher pay or continued their education. I remained in a comfortable-uncomfortable position.

My lack of confidence and complete avoidance of speaking in front of a group caused me to lose out on potential opportunities in my career. I ended up leaving the corporate world. In some ways I felt a relief of not comparing myself to others that went on ahead to flourish in their careers. I noticed my thoughts that were limiting me were definitely turning my life in a direction I never would have dreamed years ago.

Where was the Darla that had dreams of being an artist?

Four years after my divorce from my daughter's father, I got remarried to a man who I thought was my prince charming. He was a gentleman through and through. He had it all. He was tall and handsome, attentive to my needs and accepted my daughter. However, as I found out a year after we were married, he wasn't who I thought he was. There were problems that came up that I didn't know how to handle. I thought if I showed him more love, I could help with his anger issues. At least I did at the time, and the counselor gave both of us hope. We continued to live in the Pacific Northwest while my daughter was attending school. Once my daughter was pretty much grown and had headed off to continue her education at the University of Oregon, I was an empty nester. I was only 39 years old.

I'd grown tired of the constant cloudy skies and rainy days in the Portland area. According to the weatherman, the upcoming winter was tagged to be one of the wettest on record. So, when my husband had a convention in Arizona, I happily tagged along to get some much-needed vitamin D in the form of sunshine. I was glad to get out of the rain for a few days. I had some time to myself, so I decided to go shopping and a little exploring around the area. I hopped into the rental car and started driving with no particular destination in mind. After about 20 minutes of sight-seeing I found myself on the outskirts of Phoenix in a nice community. Near the center of the town was a man-made lake with a big fountain in the center of the lake that sprayed water high into the sky. It looked like what I could imagine an oasis in the middle of the desert would look like. I parked the car and took a walk that was leading me into the desert. The hills were covered with the biggest cacti I'd ever seen. I learned the cactus was called "Saguaro" and they can grow up to be over 40ft tall.

Taking several steps into the open desert, a rush of feelings came flooding over me and I started to cry. I wasn't sure why, but I couldn't remember ever feeling quite this way before. I'd felt a spiritual presence around me as the hot dry air filled my lungs. The sound of the desert was different. The silence was a different kind of silence. I wanted to fall on my knees and cry but didn't for obvious reasons of the harsh ground. The birds sounded different, almost tropical, and I could see the mountains as they weren't covered up by all the trees like they are in the North West. It was beautiful.

I wiped the tears out of my eyes and stood there looking at the clear outline of the mountains around me. I knew then I wanted to live there.

Once I felt I'd soaked up enough beauty of the desert, I made my way back to the rental car. As I was pulling out of the parking lot, a small sign across the street caught my attention. It was a for sale sign advertising "lot for sale," a direction arrow, and a phone number. I followed the sign and stopped at the lot. Yes, I knew I wanted to live here. The land had a stunning view and there were several giant Saguaro cacti standing tall on the large lot. I could visualize a stunning home of southwestern architecture, a negative edge pool and most importantly I could still feel the spirit of the desert! I felt inspired which is something I hadn't felt in a long time.

A few months later we'd sold our home in Oregon and were unloading our belongings into a rental house close to our lot in Arizona. We were getting ready to build the new home I'd designed, and had been working with the builder via emails and phone calls before we moved as to save time. I was looking forward to seeing our home being built, making some new friends and having a fresh start.

My marriage was full of challenges and dysfunction. I'd never known anyone who had anger as a normal mode of operation. I believed this move would make everything better.

Early one morning I was doing paperwork in my home office and noticed a newspaper that I'd put aside to get back to the article on the front of the Arizona Republic newspaper. I had some time before meeting with the builder that morning, so I picked it up and started thumbing through it from back to front. Once I turned to the front page, I'd remembered the reason I'd saved it. The headline read "Local Millionaire Pays No Taxes." The article included information about a new book, *Rich Dad, Poor Dad,* by Robert Kiyosaki. I went to the local bookstore that same day and bought the book. I read through it in just a couple hours. I couldn't believe what was going through my head.

I wanted to stop building my dream home on the dream lot.

We were making plenty of money with the self-employed business, but the quarterly taxes were more than we used to make in a single year. I took a check into my husband's office to pay the taxes and I remember saying to him, "What would you do if we didn't have to pay these high taxes anymore? What if you could retire in just a few years?"

We were into consumerism, spending our money on things that didn't give us any returns. It was one big party, thinking buying "things" would solve our problems. We weren't living beyond our means; we had the money to spend, but we weren't structured properly for the business, and we weren't thinking about the future. I left the book on my husband's desk.

The next day we stopped the building of the house and agreed to look for something already built that was a nice, yet conservative home. We sold the lot for a loss, but it was a good loss.

I remember when reading his book, Robert Kiyosaki mentioned finding a mentor, so I did. I ended up with what I believe to be one of Robert's rich dads. He, John Burley, was a personal friend of Robert's who happened to live in Arizona as well.

Mr. Burley has an extensive financial background and was a real estate investor. I learned a lot from John. In fact I started buying investment houses and we became debt free, including our home and cars in less than 2 years. I ended up working for the Burley organization as a coach helping other new student investors find their freedom.

Shortly after this, Robert Kiyosaki was asked to be on the *Oprah Winfrey Show* to talk about his popular book. The Oprah Show was looking for people who could be testimonials for Robert to be on the show. I submitted my story about how I turned our financial future around after reading the book. The very next morning I was surprised when I received a phone call from one of Oprah's producers. Her name was Jennifer, and she asked me a few questions about my experience after reading the *Rich Dad, Poor Dad*. She said she would contact me if they thought they wanted any more information from me. Several hours later, the phone rang again, and Jennifer told me they wanted to come to my home on Saturday, just two days away! Of course, I said YES! I was excited out of my mind and scared at the same time!

Oprah's producer, Jennifer, along with a sound guy and camera man showed up to my home early Saturday morning to film my story. When the interview started, I pretty much froze. The noise in my head was deafening. It was a loud roar of, "Don't embarrass yourself again! See you're doing it already! You can't do this! What's wrong with you?!" Thankfully Jennifer and the crew were patient and helped me by prompting me on what to say. I was finally able to tell my story; no prompting or words being put into my head from the crew. It was a long day and I wasn't sure if I would hear back from them or not. I was actually ok with that because I was exhausted.

Two days later I found myself in Chicago on Monday morning, all expenses paid. I was picked up at the airport by a chauffeur, was, driven to the Omni Hotel for the night. Bright and early the next day Oprah's limo service would be taking me to the Harpo Studio building. I found out there were only two people picked out of hundreds who submitted their story and I was one of the two.

SHOW TIME ...

Too nervous to eat, I started my day with just a cup of coffee with about 4 teaspoons of sugar. The limo arrived right on the dot. As I jumped in the car, I saw I was sharing a ride. Financial advisor Jean Chatzky, who was a regular guest on the morning news shows, was also going to be on the show. I was nervous, really nervous. So instead of being outgoing, the person I really am inside, I was quiet, and barely said a thing to her other than "Hi, it's nice to meet you," sort of thing.

Once at Harpo Studios, I was ushered into the green room with Jean, where the staff did Ms. Chatzky's makeup and hair. They gave me a quick touch up, too, making me feel a little less self-conscious. Jennifer, the producer, came in to tell me a little about what was going to happen on the show and what was expected of me. I was going to be sitting in the front row along with the other person that was picked, a fireman, while our stories were going to be shown on national television. My story was played on the big screen in the studio to the audience. When my story was finished playing, Oprah asked me a couple questions. I was really nervous (it felt like an out of body experience). I wasn't myself, but I mustered up the confidence to answer the only question I can remember. When Oprah asked me, "Darla, can you tell me what it feels like now that you've changed the way you were living?" My answer to Oprah was and still is "Freedom ... for as long as I can remember, I feel free for the first time in my life." But at that very moment on national TV, I couldn't have felt any less free. I felt frozen and felt as if I was out of my body ... my ears ringing. The time went quickly and before I knew it the show was over. I was given a coffee mug, and Oprah had signed a thank you letter to me for being on the show. In minutes the limo pulled up and rushed me to the airport heading back to Arizona.

After the show, I received lots of attention from my Real Estate colleagues, and viewers of the national show. My husband and some friends were pushing me to take advantage of the opportunity, but I didn't want the attention. I wanted to crawl into a hole because my limiting beliefs about myself and the self-sabotaging thoughts that kept repeating "I wasn't good enough." I didn't like talking about the show or my accomplishments. But I knew in my heart I'd missed a once in a lifetime chance that would have been good for my family, good for me and especially good for my future. It could have been an opportunity for me to be free.

3
My Florida Hurricane

*Be willing to get uncomfortable
with your uncomfortable life.*

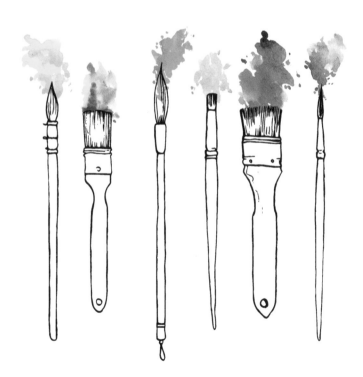

Breathing In ...

One ... two ... three ... whhh ... whhh ... whhh ...

Breathing Out ...

One ... two ... three ... shhh ... shhh ... shhh ...

A rhythmic discipline of breathing over and over again until my lungs, body, arms, legs and feet are in complete alignment. I'm no longer aware of the struggle, or the negative self-talk.

Breathing in ...

One ... two ... three ... whhh ... whhh ... whhh ...

Breathing Out ...

One ... two ... three ... shhh ... shhh ... shhh ...

All else disappears, the wholeness and awareness of being one with the Divine Source encompassing my body. Breathing together as One. This is when my clarity and creativity rush into my mind.

I was taught this breathing technique by a running coach. Before learning this, I struggled too long to get into an easy stride, and most importantly the rhythm. When this rhythm happens, the running becomes secondary. I am almost unaware of the physical act of placing one foot in front of another. At first, I hear the sound of my feet hitting the concrete below me. Once I'm in rhythm, the pounding sound of my feet is just a faint background noise. This is optimal for me; no pain or effort, just breezing through the thick heavy air of Florida in the summer. This is my runner's high.

I hadn't called myself a runner for several years. Too many moves to different cities in different states, and too many dreams thwarted. I didn't feel like running. I'd stopped taking care of that part of myself. I'd just moved to Tampa, Florida with my husband to chase another one of his dreams. I had a constant feeling that I was living in the in-between, no longer living my old life, yet not living my current life either. I knew no one, was as far away from my family and friends that was humanly possible living in the U.S. mainland, and was mostly in solitude. I was lonely and to be honest with myself, I was afraid.

My now grown daughter was living in San Francisco working and going to school to become a Nurse Practitioner. She knew I had just moved and didn't know anyone, so she told me about Facebook being a cool way to keep in contact with friends. I signed up and created my first online profile. I missed my daughter. She's my only child and we were always close to one another, especially since it had been just her and me for several years. We'd been participating in the annual Susan Komen Race for the Cure event in San Francisco the past couple years. This year I was across the country and it was obviously too far to drive down for the weekend. I'd seen the Race for the Cure event posted on Facebook and it was scheduled to be in Saint Petersburg, Florida, just a town away from where I was living. I decided it would be good for me to go. It's for a good cause and it's personal as my mother was a survivor of the big "C."

I knew I would have to run by myself, but I was okay with that and was actually glad. I'd forgotten how running clears my head and my thoughts become less. Sometimes I'd even have a sense of clarity rush in.

I impulsively clicked the button on the info page and signed up for the event. However, what I didn't know at the time was two things: 1) I didn't realize my friends on Facebook could see I'd signed up for the run and, 2) I'd accidentally signed up for the 10k, not the fun one-mile walk/run.

Yikes—is putting it mildly!

I'd never run that far in one run before! I calculated that I had to run 6.3 miles. I hadn't been running regularly for a long time and I was thinking I'd be lucky to run for 1/2 mile without stopping. Being in Florida, even a mile felt like a very long workout because of the extreme heat and humidity. I'd never actually run more than 4 miles in one stretch before and definitely not that long of a race. It was August in Florida. What was I thinking?

Before I moved to the Sunshine State, I had no idea how much I was able to sweat. It wasn't a pretty picture that's for sure. Seeing myself in the mirror, after doing a slow jog around the Tampa Bay shoreline, gave me a shock and I was depressed over how bad I looked and how old I felt.

Being in Florida in the summer I experienced a new kind of sweating, like I never had before. It was as if my body turned on a faucet and every single pore was turned on full blast! I soaked through my clothes as soon as I got dressed in the morning. My hair was completely out of control, plump and frizzy is putting it mildly. Ugh! The humidity and heat felt worse than the summers in Arizona. At least in Arizona, my hair still looked good and jumping in the pool always cooled me off. Maybe I'd just keep a low profile and just do the short walk or even cancel all together. But then the kicker was I'd seen what my friends had written on my Facebook page. They wrote things like,"How's the training going for the 10k? Congrats for doing the run!"

Oh crap! My Facebook friends had noticed and are wanting to know how I'm doing with training to run a race! Peer pressure.

Yes, I succumbed to their prodding me. But mostly I didn't want to feel like a failure. I didn't want to disappoint my daughter or myself again. I hopped into the car and drove 3.2 miles from my front door. That's how far I had to run, there and back, to be able to make the 10k distance. The drive didn't seem that far. I began my training the next morning, in Tampa, in Old Hyde Park. My street was lined with huge trees making a canopy covering the sky with long strands of what looked like heavy chains of moss, reaching down off the big branches towards the sidewalks. This caused the air to be thick, heavy and still. I imagined them growing faster enveloping the whole neighborhood, covering the streets and even the stately houses.

Not a chance for even a slight breeze to wave by. It was suffocating.

Two weeks later, I'd found my stride. I was feeling fairly confident that I was actually going to be able to run the race, maybe even finish it. Just one month to go, I'd found some clarity and the sense of well-being when I found my easy meditative stride. My thoughts became very clear and creative solutions came to me. On this particular day I was creating a course for a women's creativity retreat I'd been working on with my friend, Meridian, who I'd known from my home town of Ashland, Oregon.

Clear-minded, I'd just finished a perfect creativity segment for the retreat in my head. I was really excited about what I was planning because this was for me. I hadn't done anything that was creative in a really long time and I was close to having the curriculum finalized before we were ready to advertise it.

Breathing In ...

One ... Two ... three ... whhh ... whhh ... whhh...

Breathing Out ...

One ... two ... Three ... shhh ... shhh ... shhh ...

Suddenly a voice in my head, very clear and loud said, "Who do you think you are?"

"You can't do that!" "You're not qualified to teach that!"

I was instantly deflated. I stopped dead in my tracks and almost immediately, what seemed as a 2nd voice, popped in and said, "Don't we both want the same thing for Darla? We want her to be happy. Can't we work together?"

I actually thought I may have been talking out loud to myself by the Bay that day, and, honestly, I don't know if I was or not. I looked around to see if anyone was looking at me as if I was a little crazy. To my relief no one was looking at me, but it really didn't matter. What did matter, was that I realized the voice telling me that I couldn't do what I wanted to do was a very familiar one. It was a voice that had been sabotaging my plans and my dreams for a very long time.

Feeling emotional and defeated, I needed to go home. My feet were heavy as I turned my body towards my street. It felt like I'd put my tail between my legs, with my head down, putting one foot in front of the other, and slowly lumbering. By the time I reached the top of my stairs I could barely turn the knob of the front door. I was in a dazed state of mind, feeling not good enough, and broken again. All I could hear in my head was, "You can't do that. Who do you think you are?" But something was different this time. This time the negative voice didn't seem like it was from me. It felt like it was someone else telling me I should quit, and that I was a failure.

Once inside, I passed on my normal shower ritual and flopped myself down on the sofa, sweat dripping. I didn't care. On the table next to the sofa was a notebook. I picked it up along with my pen. I felt an uncontrollable urge to find out more about the negative voice, and what she'd told me that day.

Who was she and why did she show up now? Why did I feel she was separate from me?

I just sat for a while. I have no idea how long. I just sat, still sweating. Still feeling a bit stunned and sad with another plan squelched. I was letting the negative voice in my head sabotage my dreams again. I noticed how easily I seemed to slide right back into defeat. The thoughts though weren't mine. Yet, they are mine and I'd taken them on as truth.

I started thinking to myself how little potential I had to follow my dreams, and at this very moment, that sabotaging voice in my head was right. I'd let myself and others down over and over again. At least that's what the she wanted me to believe. She. Yes, I knew it was a female and for some reason I felt it wasn't me. But it was oh so familiar; it was hard to separate myself from her. It was like she was a clever saboteur, like an undercover spy, looking for any opportunity or evidence she could use against me to stop me. But why?

I wrote down the words that came flying loudly into my head.

Loser!

I'm not smart enough.

My life sucks.

People talk behind my back.

No one likes me.

I'm tired.

Don't embarrass yourself.

You're not qualified.

You don't have the right education.

You're too old.

You're Ugly.

Fat.

It's a good thing you have me to protect you.

Best to play it safe.

Go take a shower! You stink!

Over the next several days I became obsessed with this voice—with her voice. I felt I had to know more, and I felt she wanted me to know more about her.

Something inside me was nudging me to go ahead and separate her from myself. Then I remembered the 2nd voice, the voice who said, "Can't we work together?" That's all the permission I needed to delve into a project of separating myself from the Saboteur, who seems to always be in the shadows waiting to pounce on me whenever I ventured out of my uncomfortable comfort zone.

I'd definitely be safer if I'd just follow her lead and quit having these silly dreams that I'd never manifest. But I was growing old of "safe" ... I was growing old of "living in the in-between" and I wanted to live an engaged life.

The problem was, I believed her.

I hated her.

I wanted to crawl into bed, pull the covers over my head and never come out. I couldn't even do that well, because it was so stinking hot. Who was this person inside of me? I know in my heart it wasn't me. The real me was not like this!

4

Swimming in the Deep End

Remember she is not me ...
Breathe ...
Breathe ...
Breathe ...

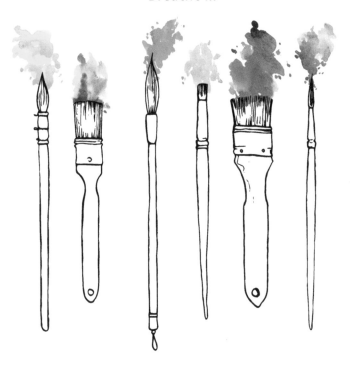

Why is it that I can so easily believe the worst? Why is it that I can embrace the negative yet dismiss and discard the good? Good question.

These past few months I'd been pretty much in isolation again. I'd become familiar with being alone, but this time it felt lonelier. I think it was just the perception I had that was different because of the three thousand miles between myself, my family and friends. I couldn't easily get in my car and drive home. Besides, we had only one car in Florida and I was left with no transportation much of the time. Not knowing anyone in a new city all the way across the country was hard. All I had was me and my thoughts.

Besides training for my first 10k race, I'd taken on another project. This one was even more personal than an accomplishment of crossing the finish line. Diving deep within my mind felt a little bit like swimming with the sharks.

This was something unknown, feeling like I could be way over my head and yet I knew it would be life changing. I needed to end the negative thinking. I knew being negative wasn't me and I was so tired of starting and stopping things I wanted to do. It was bad enough that I was married to someone with wild mood swings, I was listening to my inner saboteur as well. I knew I couldn't change others' well-defined unhealthy behaviors, so I thought the least I could do was to change what I'd been accepting from myself.

I had to take responsibility for myself. I felt once I looked in the mirror and into the eyes of the saboteur inside me that life would never be the same. The scary thing for me was I was unsure how it was going to end up. My life could get massively worse and I could sink into the depths of depression, self-loathing, and feeling totally worthless. Yet I knew if I continued on the same path I'd been on for years, nothing would change. Now I've stepped on to a new path and am finally determined to follow through and follow my soul nudges. I feel that I may actually like myself and be happy. Maybe even forgive and love me.

I had to trust my intuition, or nudges from my soul, and I knew in my heart this negative voice wasn't me. I didn't like this person that kept me from doing what I wanted to do. It was declared Saboteur Day. I was dedicating my entire day or more to her, proceeding carefully with plenty of oxygen to keep me afloat. I really did hate her. She was arrogant, rude, mean, a know-it-all and at the same time, weak and afraid. I felt I needed to get to know her intimately, otherwise nothing would ever change, and that just wouldn't do anymore. I was reminded of the saying, "Keep your friends close and keep your enemies closer." I was done with being bullied and criticized. I was tired of it; was desperate to find myself, my real self, and start a new life outside of living in the in-between.

So it begins, my journey to know everything about my inner saboteur. I needed to know all about who said this negative self-talk to me. Who was she? She wasn't me. I kept telling myself that and I needed to cut her out of my life once and for all. I'm not exactly sure how I was feeling at the time, probably because I was in some kind of trance, almost an out of body feeling ... somewhat detached and ready to dive deep into the depths of my saboteur's mind.

I'd gathered a fair amount of knowledge from researching abusive behavior, going to marriage counselors and learning how the mind works (or doesn't work) over the past couple years. Since I'd felt such a strong soul nudging the day I was running, I was driven more than ever to take this unwanted part of me, separate it from me and focus on this part specifically.

I sat with my hand poised to write. I was feeling somewhat like how I imagine a private detective would be handling an in-depth "fragile" interview, leaving no stones unturned before coming to a conclusion.

I'm not sure if it took a few minutes or an hour. Time seemed to stand still with me just sitting staring at the blank page before I decided to grab a different notebook. The one I'd started with had no lines on the page, it was too freeform for her. The lined pages were easier to keep structured. I started writing whatever came to mind. I already knew she was older than me, but she wouldn't reveal her age. I paused. It reminded me of what my grandmother said when she was asked how old she was. "Age is just a number, and mine is unlisted."

I think she wants to be older, so she has authority over me. She's shorter than me. I'm 5'8" and she thinks I'm too tall. She says she's the perfect height for a woman: 5'6". Hmmm ... She's thin, skinny is more like it, not an ounce of extra fat on her body anywhere. She attributes this to her proper eating habits and walking. She told me it's best to eat properly, taking small bites from small portions of food. Always. She prefers eating only on fine china and never eats off paper plates; using paper towels instead of cloth napkins or eating with plastic cutlery is acceptable. Never. She's obviously embarrassed and disgusted with me. She reminded me that I was sent to Charm School when I was just entering my teens. I can't stand her. I'm starting to feel like a loser.

I've written down everything that popped into my mind with my sloppy handwriting. She pops in and tries to get me to write like I was taught in school. I pause and keep on writing like I feel like. I'm not letting her bully me, and I can clean it up later. She continues on. Her hair is short, above her shoulders, just a smidgen below the bottom of her earlobes. The proper length. A woman over forty should never have long hair, it looks ridiculous and it's time to grow up. Color? It's medium ash brown (I'd call it a bit drab) with an intentional perfection of waves that always seem to stay in place. Her eyes are green. Maybe they're green because she secretly envies me.

Ha!

Her favorite colors are navy blue and taupe. She wears them like a uniform. No need to put on 5 different outfits to fit a mood ... that's just plain silliness. I am noticing something a little unexpected. Her shoes are red. Yes, they are conservative 2in. mid-heel, rounded-toe classic pumps, but they are most certainly RED! Interesting. Her favorite is a suit, taupe of course, with a mid-knee length slightly A-line skirt, and a button-down jacket. Her only jewelry is a simple strand of pearls, real ones though, never ever anything but certified authentically real. No earrings. They bring unneeded attention.

So, I know pretty much what she looks like from her description and I start to draw her on a page in my unlined notebook. I sketched her fairly quickly. I didn't really care what she looked like, so I gave myself permission to put my "I'm not good enough to draw" on hold for the few minutes. I knew I'd finished with her when I paused for a moment putting down the pencil and picked up the red pen for her shoes. Under my breath I whispered ... "Finished!"

There she was staring right back at me from the page. I saw her for the first time. I just sat there staring back at her.

I'm not sure how long I sat in silence, or how long she stared back at me. I had to stop.

I needed a break. By now I'd come to the conclusion that I was right in needing to know all I can about my saboteur and her personality. She was not me and this was definitely feeling like it's going to be a project.

"My Saboteur"

5
Getting Intimate

Getting to know someone makes them real.
When they become real, they can be changed.

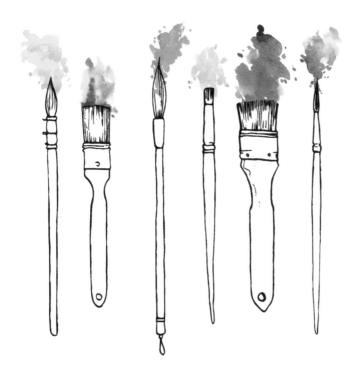

For the next two days I avoided the project. I needed to focus on my running and clearing my head. I was feeling a little uneasy. The not knowing where this was going to end up was honestly scary for me. When I ran, I felt powerful and free, it's probably the only time I felt this way.

I was drawn to know more about what makes her tick. I confirmed on my last few days running that I needed to know all there is about my Saboteur, everything she doesn't like about me, everything else she doesn't like, and what she did like ... as if she were a real person.

In order to know someone intimately we really have to know all about them. So when I came back to the project, I eased in by asking what she doesn't like. Which would probably be everything. I've a pretty good idea what she's going to say and seriously, I can't imagine what she would like. Suspiciously, I believe she's looking forward to this.

Funny how when you know you need to do something, especially when it's ultimately going to be good for you, you can put it off. I went back and forth a few days before I actually sat back down in my writing spot starring at the new blank page.

I had taken on the task of separating my internal personalities, building one trait upon the other until a fully developed person that wasn't me, although an intimate part of me, felt a bit daunting.

I urged her. "Tell me everything you don't like ... I'll make it easy and start with food."

Suddenly the foods she disliked (that's putting it mildly) came flowing through my pencil. Things like, hamburgers, pizza, any type of food that requires no knives, forks or spoons ... basically, any food that's widely accepted by the masses to be eaten with hands. Her rare exceptions are cookies while she sips on her cup of tea. Of course, the cookies are small, never gooey or crumbly and she also will eat small high tea finger sandwiches, crust free of course with pinky finger poised.

My paper was looking like a shopping list with things like, beer, soda pop, spaghetti, pre-made deserts, fried foods of any kind, most cheese, pancakes, french-toast, syrup, cake, ice cream (except for sorbet as a small portion pallet cleanser). She's strict on portion size, nothing ever any bigger than what could fit within the palm of her hand. Not the size of her palm, but it needs to fit within her hand. That's at least ¼" open space all the way around. Of course, she has unusually small hands.

I switched from one topic of dislikes to another, just letting it flow. Once the flow stopped, I asked myself the question, "What makes a person a person?" Every aspect of a person, with myself and my Saboteur was my answer. I thought of a life-wheel I'd seen before. It's a simple tool that helps to visualize all the areas of life that are important to create a balanced life. It can show us where we have unbalance.

Most of the wheels I've seen or used had these main components: Spiritual, Community, Money, Relationships/Family, Career, Health, Personal Growth (learning), Self-image. So I decided to go on from here, using the wheel as a guide for the things she doesn't like.

Spiritually, my Saboteur doesn't like any of what she calls "woo-woo" religions. If it isn't a conservative, long standing, and a recognized Christian religion she doesn't trust it and finds it to be evil.

Community? She doesn't like people in her community that are unemployed, homeless, ones that protest on the streets (organized or not), hippies, or youth running around without supervision. She doesn't like anyone pushing the boundaries of a comfortable, conservative community. Those all scare her.

Money ... she doesn't like wasting it.

Relationships/family ... she doesn't reveal anything about this subject.

Careers ... Actors are overpaid and overrated. People who are unorganized drive her crazy. She dislikes fat people and those who don't pay their own way. Personal Growth, well that's for other people. Self-Image? No comment.

A new list of words flows from the lead in my pencil: No rock music, country, music, alternative, but she occasionally will tolerate some limited jazz. She doesn't like sitcoms, teenage movies, comedies, war movies, thrillers, westerns, action, science fiction, superhero, crime, epic, disaster, martial arts, animated ... whew!

That's a lot of opinions!

She also doesn't like trucks, 4-wheel drives, small cars, SUV's, old cars, most foreign cars and if the car isn't white or occasionally silver, she doesn't like them. She doesn't like pets of any kind. They are too messy, smelly, loud, dirty germ carriers. She doesn't like it when people dress casually. That's for home, not for work or going out in public.

Honestly towards the end, I think I was making things up. But I was on a roll and they were based on how I thought she'd be if she were a person standing in front of me. I wrote until there was nothing left to say.

I'm finding the deeper I go with her the more I feel she's separate from me. She's not me and in so many ways she's the exact opposite of me. Yet she's been a big part of my life for as long as I can remember.

6

The Saboteur Takes a Turn

I can't stop with just what she doesn't like.
I need to know what she likes, too.

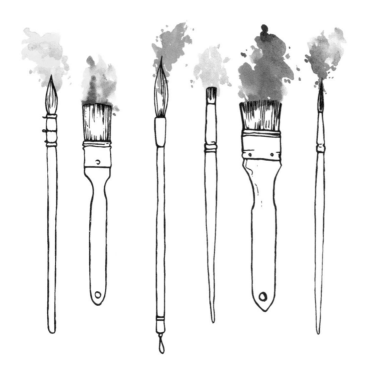

I start with easy questions that are in the same order as her dislikes, since I know how much she dislikes disorder. Starting with the kind of foods she likes, what's her favorite type of music to listen to and so on. She seems hesitant with this line of questioning and is slower with the answers. I imagine she was as unprepared for this as I am, and she doesn't like this kind of attention. But I persisted and wrote down every single item in list form in my notebook. I intentionally switched to writing with a pen. I knew she liked this, and I almost saw the corner of her mouth slightly turn up.

She loves classical music, as she pretty much had already told me earlier when I was listing her dislikes. She prefers the classics of Bach and Mozart as well as some of the tunes from a good Broadway show. Incidentally her favorite show of all time is *Phantom of the Opera.*

She is a creature of habit, which brings her comfort. For breakfast she'll have a poached egg cooked medium, a cup of very hot English breakfast tea and a perfectly even sliced banana. If she snacks at all it would again include a cup of tea and a small dish of applesauce or yogurt. Lunch pretty much consists of a bowl of cream of tomato soup, sometimes with small oyster crackers on top, or a salad with water packed, low salt tuna and a sliced tomato. Dinner is half of a small chicken breast, rice and broccoli or green beans. Dessert—tapioca pudding is her favorite as it reminds her of her mother.

I continued to list all things I believed she would like. She's feeling more separate from me than when I first started this project. I could clearly see her as completely separate and different from me. It was getting easier and easier for me. I actually started to enjoy this process. I felt better about myself and felt a sense of power return. I could visualize her in my minds-eye as she walked out the door with her perfectly placed hair, mauve lipstick, mascara, no eyeshadow or eyeliner ever, the meticulously pressed suit, perfectly fit, in her favorite shade of taupe. The strand of pearls was almost glowing, and I'm still surprised that her sensible shoes are red. She opened her car door, stepped in, closed the door, made her habitual adjustments and the taillights of the silver Mercedes sedan shine red as she slammed on the brakes for an idiot who's speeding down the street. A bit rattled she speeds off, too! Hmmm ... I thought she said she didn't like foreign cars.

One of the main things I noticed is that she seems very organized. It's her way of controlling things. Everything has its place. All the bills are paid before they become due. She makes lists that she actually uses and crosses each item off until the last one has a simple line through it. She then folds it neatly and places it in the recycle bin. Her small private back yard is perfectly manicured with no sign of a dropped leaf on the ground.

I looked around my desk and saw a mess, what looked like chaos, and it was. My desk looked like a bomb went off inside it, on top of it and has spilled over onto the floor. I can't imagine what it would be like to be that meticulous. That image quickly goes away because of all the other attributes she has. She's so unlike me and not who I know I'm supposed to be like or live like. Of course, my husband would have loved me being more like my Saboteur. They'd probably get along in so many ways. They are both judgmental for one. Except for the anger ... my Saboteur isn't angry ... she's just scared and uncomfortable.

She isn't very social and prefers to be alone most of the time. She likes being taken care of by hiring a weekly housekeeper, (which took her months to find the exact right one, that knows how to clean everything without missing one spot of dust.) She occasionally takes the white glove out of the top-drawer dresser and sits it on the dining table, just to make sure the housekeeper knows she's being watched. She has her hair colored every 21 days exactly to the day and has added an assistant to help her run errands that she'd rather not do.

I found myself just sitting, no longer writing. I was imagining her in my mind's-eye and I was compelled to continue just watching her.

I was starting to feel comfortable that I know this part of me. This person was not me, but has held me captive for many, many years now—too many. I've forgotten how many things I've wanted to do, but didn't do them, because of her. I had forgotten how many times I ended up feeling unworthy, unhappy, and not good enough because of her.

People can fall into the "I'm not good enough" dialogue because of television, movies, bad dates, bad marriages and abusive relationships. Trying to keep up with the Jones ... now on the list is the big one of Social Media. Even a relatively successful person can fall into the "I'm not good enough" dialog. I've seen it in some of my friends.

On and on it can go. Seemingly everywhere you look. Because you become conditioned to look for evidence that you are not enough. You look for the negative; you look for the proof that you were right about yourself. The voice gets louder, bigger and before you know it, you can become frozen, lack self-confidence, have low self-worth, become painfully shy and a recluse, and even in some cases you can begin stuttering or take on other physical manifestations.

After spending the time with my Saboteur, something seems to have shifted in me. I noticed I hadn't actually heard her voice as much.

The word "weave" came into my head a few times while I was working with my Saboteur. I thought of her hair, but had to immediately disregard that, as it didn't seem to fit anywhere. I let it go.

7
Critic vs Saboteur

Be willing to let go of perceived beliefs.

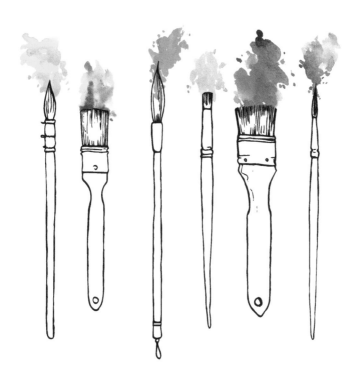

When I casually mentioned the Saboteur to people, most were scratching their head, wondering what I was talking about? They didn't even have to ask the question, the look on their faces was enough for me to want to stop the whole project. It's not a surprise when you mention your Critic, inner critic, or even the "shadow" most people know what you're talking about.

People weren't sure what I was talking about and honestly, I wasn't sure why I was supposed to call "IT" the Saboteur. However, my intuition or divine intervention (which is a more accurate account) was loud and clear on the naming of the inner critic the Saboteur.

I did some research and began to understand why I call this inner critic a Saboteur. The inner critic talks shit to us, yes, just like the Saboteur does, but often the inner critic stops with a few critical opinions. In my case, I noticed it had gone beyond the little voice of supposedly constructive criticism and takes it to the next level of sabotaging my plans. I had actually stopped dreaming of what I wanted to do. The Saboteur had become a part of my psyche, a part of my mindset that was more dominant than not.

I started to recall how many times I'd had ideas and things that I knew would bring me joy and accomplishment only to have been squelched by sabotage. It definitely felt like sabotage. For a really, really long time I'd blame others for my lack of follow through and action. Yes, I was in an unhealthy long-term relationship; yes, I'd had others to blame, but I was the one who stopped myself most of the time. I didn't want to take responsibility. I had a Saboteur living inside of me that kept taking over my mind. It was the Saboteur's fault, not mine.

I knew I was better than that, not that I was better than other people, but I felt I had more potential than just living in the in-between and feeling handcuffed all the time. I felt like what I wanted to do was somehow being guided by someone or something bigger than myself. However, I kept having to deal with what I felt was real sabotage, a part of myself I didn't like.

Part of me wanted to leave my unhealthy relationship for a better life. The other part was too afraid of the unknown and the "what if" scenario of being alone.

Part of me wanted to be healthy, in shape and active, and the other would binge on junk food and tv.

Part of me wanted to stand up for myself and stop others' judgement of me. The other part of me said don't rock the boat.

Part of me wanted to be an artist and the other part believed there was too much competition and I'd never be good enough.

Part of me wanted to be free and travel the world. The other part wanted to stay safe because the world was too dangerous and what would other people say behind my back.

Part of me wanted to live at the beach. The other part said I could never afford it.

Part of me wanted a divorce and to be free. The other part said it would be too hard, too dangerous. I would be alone and the thought of being alone scared me.

Part of me wanted to have more close friends. The other part said no one likes me.

Part of me wanted to be a teacher. The other part said I wasn't smart enough or educated enough.

Part of me wanted to be an author. The other part said I can't write.

And so it goes on and on.

In doing research I found that by definition, a saboteur is a person who makes a mess of a situation on purpose. Was I my own saboteur?

So, what is the inner saboteur really? The inner saboteur is a part of our psyche. "Parts" are like subpersonalities, which have been a point of discussion in philosophy and psychology since ancient times.

The book, *Subpersonalities* by Rowan (1990), is a good introduction to psychological parts. I believe the first mention of a subpersonality (and a conversation with it) is said to have occurred in ancient Egypt when a man wrote a book about "a conversation with his soul."

The inner saboteur is the part of us that loves to screw things up. But why? For what purpose? I looked up the definition of Saboteur and when I read it, I knew it was the perfect fit for my inner critic, shadow, negative and stinking thinking part. I needed to start listening to my Divine guide. I'm pretty sure we all have this access to our Divine Source, we just have to put ourselves in a space where the noise and chatter stops, even for just a moment or two.

Definition of Saboteur:
(compiled from Wikipedia.org, Dictionary.com)

One who engages in sabotage is a saboteur. Saboteur is a noun that is fairly new to the English language; it was first used in the early 1900s, and it refers to a person who deliberately destroys or obstructs something.

It comes from the French word, saboteur, which really and truly means to kick something with a steel toed shoe.

The Thesaurus definitions of Saboteur

1) someone who commits sabotage or deliberately causes wrecks

Synonyms: a diversionist, wrecker

Types: sleeper, a spy or saboteur or terrorist planted in an enemy country who lives there as a law-abiding citizen until activated by a prearranged signal

Type of: destroyer, ruiner, undoer, uprooter, waster, a person who destroys or ruins, or a member of a clandestine subversive organization who tries to help a potential invader a fifth columnist, type of traitor, treasonist, someone who betrays his or her country by committing treason.

Treason—Oh boy how I can relate to this one!

8
What's in a Name?

Name your poison.

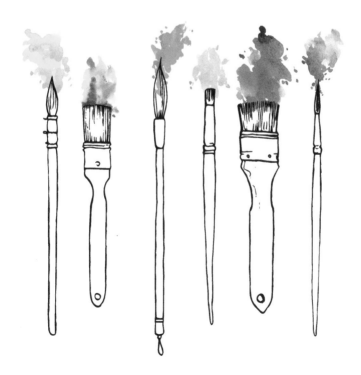

Even though I'm in the process of uncovering my inner saboteur, I know she comes from multiple sources; different people and events that took place in my life that I've unconsciously, and sometimes consciously, taken the negative on as truth about myself. These negative truths about myself come from family, intimate relationships with their own limiting beliefs and negative emotions that have formed from generations of being handed down from one person to another. Also, in my case, teachers who are unaware of the "little things" that may seem insignificant at the time (but aren't to a child). Kids can be downright mean on purpose and even our friends can say things to us that hurt. Coaches who are focused on the win of the game verses the impressionable young players. Religions with all the rules and thou shalt not ... and thou shalt do ... hold a big stick making it nearly impossible to feel worthy enough. Over time the negatives most often become habits and then you take them as our truth without really questioning them.

Taking this all into consideration, as to where, why and how, all her dislikes, negative emotions, her likes ... I'm to a point where I think need to name the saboteur. I've contemplated pretty much everything else, so I'm following the lead to give her a name. A real name, not just the Saboteur, or the Shadow, or Critic.

So, what's her name?

I stared at the drawing of her, and the words that have been written about her, wondering what her name was.

As she stares back at me, she does resemble my mom but a little younger, so my first inclination is to give her a name that reminded me of my Mom's name or something that rhymes with it. I quickly feel a nudge and decide it's not a good idea, knowing there were many people, situations and environments, aside from my mom, that made up my Saboteur. So, when looking at my Saboteur I see an up-tight, very prim and proper woman. She's driven by fear so she's very protective of herself and obviously of me as well. She's organized and very smart. She's older than me but not old enough to be my mom. Keeping these things in mind, I start surfing the internet for her name. I look up names that would have been popular in her age group. I scroll down the list going through the alphabet and finally, when I get to the N's I intuitively knew I'd found her name. Nora. At first it was my inclination to give her a name I didn't like because I didn't like her, but after about 3 seconds, I decided I needed to give her a nice name that fits her personality with no other ulterior motives. I did that because I was desperate to end the negative abusive self-talk, and those limiting beliefs about myself that I'd taken on as my truth, and not living the life I'd love to live.

The saying you can't attract bees with vinegar is so true but show them some honey, and they'll show up happy. I wanted my Saboteur to be happy, because I wanted to be happy. I wanted to heal my Saboteur because I wanted to be healed.

This process I've taken to get to know my Saboteur had at times been hard, and an intriguing journey so far. Each step has taken me deeper into my inner self, carefully looking in the mirror to see who was really looking back at me. I remember the day I'd run home after hearing the two distinctive voices and walking into the bathroom to wash off the sweat on my face. The reflection I saw in the mirror was certainly not a pretty picture; it was ugly. I didn't like who I saw looking back at me. Not because I'd just been running in the hot sticky humidity of Florida and I pretty much looked a big hot mess. I was red faced, wearing no makeup and sweat still running off my head with my hair in a wet mat of frizz. No, it was because of the negative self-talk that was sabotaging my plans again!

Today was different, there's been a shift in me that has changed my perspective of myself. I'm finding that I'm kinder to myself. I'm finding I'm having a different perspective of my Saboteur as well, especially since I've given her a name. Psychologically speaking, it's a powerful tool to name the Saboteur. It reminds me every time any negative talk shows up, even with the little ridicule, that those are not my thoughts, they are from Nora's thoughts. Habitually thinking negatively had become automatic. But no longer. Performing this step was huge in freeing myself from the self-sabotage.

What I find interesting was my feelings for Nora had shifted. I no longer hated her. I now had compassion for her. I felt sorry for her and in some weird way I felt a need to protect her.

Don't get me wrong, I felt no need to protect her misguided bullying, and ridicule she's so proficient in. Now that I know why she does what she does, it's primarily because she's afraid. I intuitively knew that fear had been the primary negative motivation because of her perceived need to protect me!

Thinking to myself, "How can I help Nora feel safe? How can I assure Nora that I will be safe?"

9
The Weave

Note to self:
Pay attention when a word or thought comes to mind when you've been meditating or when a word keeps popping back in your head. It just may be coming from the Divine.

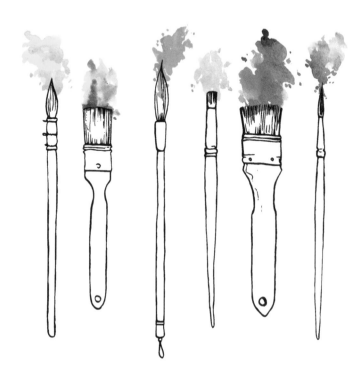

weave.

weave.

weave.

weave...

weave, weave, weave, weave, weave, weave, weave, weave, weave, weave,

weave, weave, weave, weave, weave, weave, weave, weave, weave, weave,

weave, weave, weave, weave, weave, weave, weave, weave,

weave, weave, weave, weave, weave, weave, weave, weave,

weave, weave, weave, weave, weave, weave, weave...

weave, weave, weave, weave, weave, weave, weave,

weave, weave, weave, weave, weave, weave, weave,

weave, weave, weave, weave, weave, weave, weave,

weave, weave, weave, weave, weave, weave, weave,

weave, weave, weave, weave, weave, weave, weave,

weave, weave, weave, weave, weave, weave...

weave, weave, weave, weave, weave,

weave, weave, weave, weave, weave,

weave, weave, weave, weave, weave,

weave, weave, weave, weave, weave,

weave, weave, weave, weave, weave,

weave, weave, weave, weave, weave...

weave, weave, weave, weave, weave,

weave, weave, weave, weave, weave,

weave, weave, weave, weave,

weave, weave, weave, weave,

weave, weave, weave, weave,

weave, weave, weave, weave,

weave, weave, weave,

weave, weave, weave,

weave, weave,

weave, weave,

weave, weave,

weave, weave, weave, weave, weave, weave, weave, weave, weave, weave

weave ...

This one word just wouldn't get out of my mind and I'm repeating it over and over again.

At this point, it's now jumped out of my head and onto my tongue. I found myself repeating it throughout the days out loud. Lucky for me I didn't know too many people in Florida, or I imagine someone would definitely think I was a bit of a kook!

10

Listening

Don't let who you were, talk you out of who you're becoming.

I started to feel anxious, because I was feeling trapped and somewhat defeated. I needed to get out. It was too late to run, as it was already afternoon with the temperature pushing 90 degrees. I walked down the street to the Bay and stood at the edge of the bay wall leaning over to see if I could spot a dolphin or a manatee. There was a slight breeze, yet the air was still heavy, and more oppressive than I thought it would be. The sun was bright as it reflected its rays on the water.

My mind wouldn't calm down. Thoughts were rambling on and on ... my thoughts of Nora, and what she was thinking, until I noticed them. I tried to stop all my thoughts, focusing on my breath. Breathing in deep breaths of hot humid air and releasing negativity on the exhale. Breathing in calm. Breathing out, releasing the anxiousness. While watching the water lap at the wall, I just stood there, being. Trying to be me. Whoever that is.

The beliefs about myself and the limitations I'd taken for truth for so many years no longer felt normal and taken for granted as they had in the past.

In my heart I knew the negative thoughts weren't always true, but even with that, it felt like a very hard habit to break. I'd become comfortable in my uncomfortable life. I'd taken the past events in my life that weren't positive ones for me as truth, and they'd become ingrained in my mind. Permanently ... at least that's what I'd believed up until a few weeks ago. I wasn't sure how I was going to change those unhealthy habits. Automatic habits of stinking thinking and taking them as truth can be hard to change.

Suddenly I noticed an eagle flying overhead. It landed on the sea wall just a few yards away from where I was standing. I was mesmerized by its beauty, size and apparent strength.

"Don't let who you were, talk you out of who you're becoming." What? Who said that?

A familiar voice, the one who said to me, "Don't we both want Darla to be happy?" The voice I remember so vividly that stopped me in my tracks after the voice of my saboteur put me down and tried to sabotage my efforts.

Don't let who you were, talk you out of who you're becoming. Yes! That's right. I'm no longer who I was. I've already changed merely by the fact that I've taken notice of the negative thoughts, limiting beliefs and abuse. This was me becoming someone different, someone better, someone free. A free woman. Funny how learning about yourself, diving deep and a willingness to get to know who you really are can save you and free you. If you are willing.

Intuitively I knew this voice was my Muse. I'd been working on the creativity retreat for women when I'd been shut down by sabotage, and almost instantly my inspiration and creativity guide said "No" to being shut down, not this time.

Since I'd been getting to know the negative side of myself, I felt I had no choice but to get to this part of myself as well. She was beautiful, fun, kind and smart. I knew this in my heart, and was anxious to get to know her, and learn more about myself in the process.

Muse: a spirit guide and force, creative imagination, a source of inspiration, a goddess, to think about something thoughtfully, carefully.
-Definition of Muse by dictionary.com.

I wondered as I headed back home, could the eagle have been sent to give me the message?

11
A'Muse Me Please

Letting go and learning to trust.

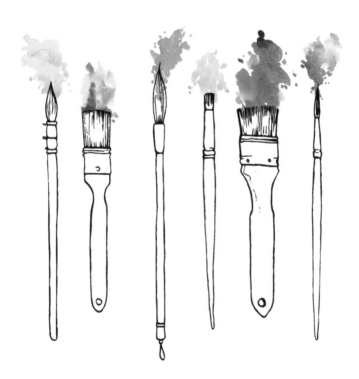

Breathing In ...

One ... two ... three ... whhh ... whhh ... whhh ...

Breathing Out ...

One ... two ... three ... shhh ... shhh ... shhh ...

All else is disappearing. Out for my morning run clearing my head this morning before sitting down with pen and paper. I remembered the words and the voice: "Don't we both want Darla to be happy?" This phrase plays over in my head, almost lyrical sounding as I rounded the corner to the street I live on. Once in the door, I immediately kicked off my running shoes, pulled off my sweaty clothes dropping them as I headed for the shower. I see the drawing of my Saboteur that's on the desk as I drop my bra on the floor. I know she doesn't approve and wants to jump off the page and put it in the laundry basket. "Sorry, not today, Nora!" I said out loud. The cold water was a bit of a shock as it ran over my head, down my shoulders and onto my feet, cooling me off and lowering my body temperature.

I had an idea that this second voice was a pretty important one. I was feeling more excited to discover my Muse (aka spiritual guide). I had a feeling this one, this part, was going to be fun. I kind of felt like this part of the project was like Christmas morning when you got up early and saw all the beautifully wrapped presents spread out well beyond the tree branches and into the room. Which one to open first? What will I find once I care-fully unwrap the beautiful package with care? Yes, that's how I felt. I was excited, and a little unsure, but happily ready to start opening her up!

I purposely wore a multicolored BoHo style oversized blouse with my favorite well-worn soft jeans, (they had holes in them before they were popular) and my go-to shoes in Florida and everywhere else I've lived, flip flops. I was comfortable and feeling good. I made a cup of coffee, poured in a well-rounded spoon of sugar with a splash of heavy whipping cream. I was ready.

I already knew this voice was a girl's, a female just few years younger than me. I had my notebook opened to a fresh page, leaving an extra blank page between my Saboteur and my Muse. I started drawing flowers and circles on the top and part way down the page, almost as if I was laying the groundwork for meeting my muse. I started asking her questions in the same order as I did with my Saboteur.

First question was, "What don't you like?" Sitting ... waiting ... I drew another flower and asked again. I began to feel maybe I wouldn't hear from her. Waiting ... waiting ... then, which seemed a lot longer than it probably was, I heard "I don't like it when you feel bad, sad or hopeless." Wow, I don't like to feel that way either! Something in common, so I feel like we are off to a good start.

"What about food you don't like?" Her answer, "I don't eat anything that has a soul: cows, cats, dogs, fish, lambs, or chickens," I got what she was saying; it was pretty much anything that would cover all animals, fish, reptiles and mammals of course. She's a vegetarian.

She told me she loves veggies, finger foods, fruit, especially papayas. Her all-time favorite was a Butterscotch milkshake. She figured she could live off of them if she were me.

This made me smile.

I felt like I had to keep my Muse somewhat under control. She's felt a bit wilder and more of a free spirit than I guess I assumed. She's certainly not the Mother Teresa type I'd imagined, that's for sure.

I've been trying to go in the exact same order of things I did with my Saboteur. Why? Is Nora trying to butt in? I turned back to Nora's page, looking at her for what felt like a long time.

Then I realized it was me who needed to let go of the control. I needed to just let it flow. To let go and trust.

What other things doesn't she like? Nothing came to me, so I decided to move on and find out what she likes besides veggies and milkshakes. I found myself writing with no lines, slanted one way then the other, spilling words all over the page. Messy, but I found it to be very comfortable and it was flowing.

Words spilling on to the page: singing, tropics, magic wand, soft smooth sheets, candy corn, love, fun, fun, fun, high, in-love, pretty toes, feather beds, dancing, discover, art, music, painting, easy going, loves colors—green, aqua, blue, purple, pink, houses, play, laughing, lightness, eyelids are the canvas of the face, peace maker, good vibes, you can do it, designer, creative, writer, inspired, flowers, studio, dogs, cats, birds, dolphins, sea turtles, diver, teacher, yoga, sharing, love, juicy blackberries, beauty, jungles, toucans, dark chocolate, meditation, adventure flying free like a blue bird over the rainbow ...

follow me ... follow me ...

I noticed I was using red ink which was such a contrast from my Saboteur's black ink and pencil lead.

I shifted from the questions and paused. I needed to get my watercolors and use them on the Muse's page. Dropping a water-filled brush with pinks, blues, yellows over the ink and words I'd just written. It was beautiful and easy flowing ... freeing actually. Then she arrived on the page. I picked up a black ink pen and followed the wet colors, drawing her outline. On her left hand her fingers turned into paint brushes and flowers, while the right was holding a house sitting next to a beautiful tree. The skirt of her dress was covered in what looks like petals or feathers. Wild thick long light-colored hair flowed off the page and she had white wings coming out of her shoulders on her back. Bright pink cheeks, colorful blue eyeshadow complimenting her deep blue eyes and of course dark pink luscious full lips. There she was, not looking directly at me though, but more at what she wanted me to see. She wanted me to go with her.

"Follow me! Follow me!" I heard her in my head.

Even though the Muse seemed a little wild to me, I instinctively knew there would be no misguided paths by following her. She was Spirit and pure Love. I could feel her energy. It's the same energy I've felt before when looking at the Ocean, or when a sunset has caught my breath because of its beauty.

I hadn't been meditating very long and I've not felt an awakening kind of energy in my body for a very long time, not like this, but it's definitely there now.

"My Muse"

12
Girl Time!

Girls just wanna have fun ...

"Great! See you then!" A few days later I found myself planning to meet my friend Meridian for lunch.

I literally didn't know anyone in Florida except my husband and a casual friend that lived several hours away on the other side of the state. I was thrilled to hear that a friend of mine from my hometown of Ashland Oregon, had just moved to Florida a few months before. Even better, she didn't live too far from me!

We would get together as often as we could, sharing the intimate details of our lives. She was safe, and we had more in common than I'd realized. She felt like what I could imagine having a sister would be like. We are both highly creative, are spiritual, love beauty in our surroundings, like to shop together, love art and we both enjoy a lovely glass of wine or two with lunch.

We'd been brainstorming on how we could hold a creative workshop together in her new town of Sarasota. This is the workshop I'd been working on in my mind the day I was shot down by my Saboteur while running by the Bay.

As I was walking to meet my friend, in the Old Hyde Park neighborhood where there are shops and restaurants within two blocks from my apartment, I found myself looking down at the sidewalk. I noticed the cracks in the cement and small plants trying to make their way above ground. The leaves of the plants are bright green against the contrast of the grey, worn cement. I didn't recognize them as weeds because of the tiny white and yellow delicate flowers on some of them. I imagine they came from the neighboring yard. In a strange kind of way, I can relate to them. The cement has been solid, hard, doing its job protecting the ground and people who are on the foot path, yet time had come for the newness and freshness to break through and reach for the sky and sunshine. Yes, it is familiar because of my Muse.

I feel she wants me to know her better, in order for me to reach for the sky, and most importantly, to follow my heart. "'Follow me! Follow me!"

I told Meridian about the download I'd been getting since the day my Saboteur shut me down when I was running on the Bay. She was definitely intrigued and wanted me to keep her posted on how it progressed. She was also encouraging and asked if she could do the same process once I was finished with it. "Of course, you can. I know I've already benefited from it (a lot)!"

It felt good to laugh and do some window-shopping together. It felt good to share our creative ideas with each other with no hesitation of being judged.

I so loved getting some much-needed girl time with my dear friend. Lunch was wonderful and a much-deserved break from being a hermit with my two opposing parts for far too long.

On my walk home the word weave started playing over in my head again. Weave, weave, weave, weave, weave, weave, weave ... on and on until my hand turned the doorknob of my apartment.

13

Creating a Job Alleviates Boredom

Get involved in activities that make you happy.

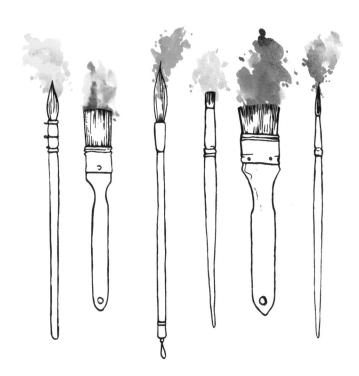

Breathing in the cool air-conditioned air was a welcoming relief from the heavy air of being outside.

Even though I'd had a shower earlier, and I only had two blocks to walk, my clothes were damp, and my hair had again already puffed out about four times in volume, reminding me of the 80's hair. I didn't care though. I'd had a great time with my friend and a glass or two of cold white wine. I was anxious to look at the pages of the project so far. Yes, it had become a project, one I'd become obsessed with.

I opened both pages so I can see both my Saboteur and my Muse at the same time. I felt good about what I was looking at. Nora's page was all neat and in order, pretty much black and white, not unlike her personality. She didn't look as harsh to me as she did when she first appeared on paper. Seeing all her words, what she doesn't like, so many things, and what she does like, not as much but equally, if not more important.

Nora liked control, liked things to be in their place, all neat and tidy. The more I got to know her, I understood her and why she'd done what she'd done. I no longer hated her for sabotaging so many of my plans and desires. I felt a deep compassion for her. I felt a deep compassion for myself.

The words "give her a job" flew in my head. Hmmm ... I'd given up on trying to understand everything about this project I felt I've been guided to do.

I'd thought I was complete with Nora. I now know why I kept sabotaging myself in the past. I knew it was out of Nora's false perception of needing to protect me, and I felt pretty good about everything at this point. She's no longer allowed to keep me from doing the things I want to do. She's no longer allowed to put unjustified fear into my mind. She's no longer allowed to tear me down and belittle me with her abusive self-talk to me.

But honestly, I didn't want this to be the end of her. I wasn't ready to throw her away or put her in a dark closet or have a burning ceremony watching her go up into smoke. I'd come to terms with her and had forgiven that part of me that had been such a big part of my life for as long as I can remember. I thought maybe this was a type of self-preservation or perhaps she just needed something else to do that can help me instead of sabotaging me.

Then "give her a job" flew into my head again.

Give her something to do that I didn't want or like to do or wasn't good at. Give her something to do that she enjoyed. I already knew everything about her, all her likes and dislikes. I also knew my likes and dislikes. One of the jobs I had several years ago was being in charge of Human Resources where I interviewed and hired people and gave performance reviews for the current staff in the office. When hiring people, I based my decisions on the company's needs (in this case, I'm the company of ME), the applicant's (aka the Saboteur, Nora) skills, their personality and probably the biggest influence of deciding one way or another was my intuition. I looked at Nora's personality profile, looking at her as if she was a real live human separate from myself. What job would she be good at if she were a real person sitting in front of me for an interview?

My intuition kicked in and the perfect job for her is to be the Company Organizer! She's so neat, very organized and doesn't like anything out of place. On the other hand, I needed help in this area of ME. This is the perfect job for her! I am feeling excited yet relaxed, and I have a sense of accomplishment and feeling complete. Nora now felt good, no longer was she threatened of being disposed of. She was complete.

She has a new purpose. She's no longer allowed to keep me from doing the things I want to do. No longer allowed to put unjustified fear and limitations into my mind.

I looked at my Muse's page. It was messy but beautiful, creative and inspiring to me. It gave me direction as my desires peeked through the layers of watercolors. For the first time in a long time I felt clear headed and excited. I took a separate piece of white paper and wrote the letters C L A I R I T Y ... cut it out and glued it on the page, her page with her name.

When growing up I disliked my name, mostly because it was different than anyone else's I knew. My middle name is Claire, which I disliked even more than my first name. I think it was because Claire was considered an old-fashioned name. But intuitively, naming my Muse Clairity felt empowering, youthful, creative and a fun Joy Seeker!

My inspiration and guide, I knew immediately my muse's job was to be a Joy Seeker. Follow me ... follow your heart.

There was no reason for me to go on any further. I was feeling really good about my Muse and the progress I'd made and at the time. I was feeling complete.

14

Weave for a Common Good

A Cohesive Whole

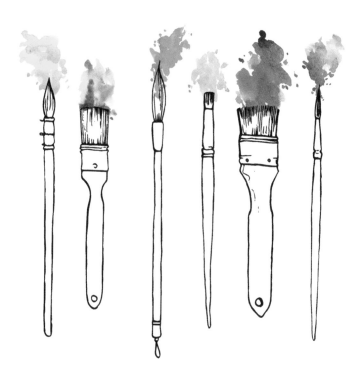

I'd noticed that Nora was silent lately. Not a peep from her which felt good—really good.

As I was reading over the words on each page, I grabbed a "breath of air" when I noticed there was a couple words that were the same on each one of their pages.

Why hadn't I noticed this before? Besides me, they also had a few things they both liked! This felt huge to me, so I began writing the things they had in common.

Nora liked classical music ... Clairity liked classical music.

Clairity liked dark chocolate ... Nora liked dark chocolate.

Nora wanted the best for me ... Clairity wanted the best for me.

Clairity liked flowers ... Nora liked roses.

Nora liked the color red ... Clairity liked red too.

Clairity wanted me to succeed ... Nora wanted me to succeed.

Clairity was from Divine Spirit ... Nora believed in the Divine.

That was enough for me ... there was common ground between the two. It didn't matter how seemingly insignificant or how big the commonality. It was enough.

Instantly the word 'weave' came flying back into my head again. Weave them together with me! The classical music and wants the best for me, and wants me to be happy and...

And it hit me!

I knew what the word weave was all about!

I'm meant to create a weave of all the parts of me together.

I had an "Ah Ha" moment! This was what the project was all about. The project needs a name, so I kept it simple and called it "The Saboteur-Muse Project."

So often you hear of your inner critic/saboteur as being discarded, or as a shadow lurking in your inner mind. Not this time ... not with me.

I noticed the word 'safe' had different meanings to Clairity and Nora. Clairity wanted me to know that I am SAFE with her in following my goals, dreams and adventures. Nora on the other hand, was afraid for me do anything based on her fears. Anything new, or what felt uncomfortable, automatically felt unsafe, so she preferred I stayed safe by not doing what my heart desired and stopped me as she has done so many times before. But I did notice they both had the word safe in common.

Instantly the word "weave" came flying back into my head.

Weave them together with ME, in the center of this project!

Now I knew for sure what the word weave was about! I'm guided to make a weave of the three parts together. But before I can dive right in, I wanted to make sure I was on the right track.

"weave: to produce by elaborately combining elements to unite a coherent whole. It is strong and hard-wearing. The tear strength is significantly higher than singular thread. Moreover, the density is increased, tearing strength of the whole is decreased."
-Definition of Weave by Merriam-Webster

Ah Ha! "To unite a coherent whole!"

This felt so right to me. So often you hear of our inner critic/ saboteur as being discarded, or as a shadow lurking in your inner mind. Not this time.

I NEEDED to make a physical weave to remind myself, my Saboteur and my Muse that together we are strong.

I didn't believe there's anything that could stop me from following my heart. I found my confidence and most importantly I loved myself, my whole self; not just part of me, but all of me! It seemed amazing to me how this has all been orchestrated by the Divine Source.

I took out three clean sheets of canvas paper I had on hand. I titled one page Nora, another with Clairity and the last was for me, so I put my name on top of the remaining blank page. On Nora's page I wrote in no particular order all the words, and some of my feelings about her on this new paper. I even doodled on the page while I was holding space until I felt it was finished.

I was ready to start on Clairity's page doing the same as I'd done for Nora's page. However, my intuition was telling me that was wrong.

What felt like out of the blue, I heard Nora's voice in my head again. She wanted to write a letter to me. Chills ran down my spine.

I moved from my comfy chair and sat at my desk, picked up a gold pen, this time in honor of Nora's request, ready to write her letter. I was a bit apprehensive because I wasn't sure what was going to end up on the page. She wrote in small cursive handwriting and very proper English:

My Dearest Darla,

I am writing to you as I believe you need to know that my intentions for you were only good ones. I needed to protect you from any further hurts, embarrassments and failures. It was my job to ensure you would always be safe and protected. I was on the look-out every moment for any possible threat to your existence and safety. Each time, day or night, I noticed any resemblance of past unwanted occurrences, I was there for you immediately. I became an expert at stopping unwanted things happening to you before they happened.

I do know now that I may have overstepped my bounds and gone a little too far. At times some of the things I have said to you were also hurtful and painful, albeit in hopes of protecting you. I am sincerely sorry for my actions and continuing to put you in these situations.

Thank you for understanding and giving me a chance to reconcile with you and still be able to help you with organizational tasks, as we both know very well how unorganized you are! For that I am deeply grateful. I am sure that someday I will understand Clairity, but at the moment I do not.

In many ways I feel free and unburdened, thank you. I do know you, (we), will be better than ever before.

Respectfully forever yours,

Nora

I found myself staring at the letter, my eyes welling up with tears. I had so much compassion for Nora, that part of me that was no longer. I had to remind myself that she was still with me, a reconciled part that now was full of compassion and self-love.

I love you, Nora.

I gave myself time to take in how I was feeling. On some level I felt a bit sad, but I wasn't even sure if that was the true feeling I was having. It may have been the hate/love relationship that I'd come to know so well from some of my real relationships with people. The dysfunctional ones. I knew that familiar feeling of sadness was not true; it was an automatic chain reaction I'd become so accustomed to. Realizing this almost immediately was a big change for me, a big healthy change. I had closure with the old Nora and a new door of possibilities and opportunity had opened for me.

I moved on to Clairity's page, doing the same as I did for Nora's page, writing everything about her I'd done before. The writing was flowery and flowy. I started to draw some of the things she likes and used different colored pens, like a rainbow. Her page was beautiful, fun, carefree, creative and resonated with me on so many levels. I yearned for this kind of lifestyle for as long as I could remember.

Since I'd given Nora the opportunity to write a letter, I gave the same to Clairity. For some reason I felt this letter wasn't meant for me, it was meant for Nora.

Hi Nora!

I'm glad we can be friends. I know how hard you have worked throughout Darla's life and did a really good job of protecting her. Now it's time for me to help her to do what she came here for. I'm not taking your place. I'm giving her the opportunity to find her true joy in life, so she can have the clarity to manifest her desires. To feel the exhilaration of being in the process. She is a born creative and I promise you she will always be safe.

Over time, you'll watch her as she focuses on mastering her emotional wellbeing. She'll have exhilarating ideas, and feelings of worthiness. She'll know that I am by her side at all times.

She's made her way to me. The feeling of clarity will be intoxicating. She'll grow to have confidence to follow her desires and inspirations.

There will be the feeling of oneness, with all of Darla, including me and you, Nora. Why does she exist? For the joy of it and the journey of selfish improvement.

Love be with you always,

Clairity

P.S. Lovely Darla, you've got this!

What could I say? I thought Clairity pretty much said everything. I felt a sense of peace for the first time in a very long time.

It was my turn to put words on the page. I hadn't written anything down for me specifically to this point. My page felt important. I was feeling soul nudges, leading me to "I AM." I wrote the words about how I felt about me in the present moment and then I proceeded to write down things I wanted for myself, my desires and goals and what inspires me. I just let the words fall upon the page, feeling the Divine and Clairity at my side.

I wrote: excited, ocean, mother, freedom, flowers, breath of fresh air, trees, pearls, creativity, friends, women, art gallery, painting, family, artist, designer, foodie, chef, home maker, clarity, peace, vulnerable, birds, transparent, outgoing, dark chocolate, green, pink, blue, purple, passionate, runner, strong, sea turtles, dolphins, Hawaii, Divine, energy, breathe in, meditate, vegetarian, beach, sand in my toes, leader, inspire, retreats, free, spirit, and on and on, cocktails, spa, travel, seafood, abundance, confident, self-assured, papaya, mangos, dream-maker, adventures, red wine, hiking, long life, healthy, nature, intimate, cherish, kindness, love ... and on and on it went until my page was full of the words that just fell onto the page.

Once I felt all three of the pages were done, I used watercolors and acrylic paints on the pages, dropping a heavily water-soaked brush with the different colors I was drawn to, based upon the individual's page. I know Nora's favorite colors are navy blue, taupe and a bit of red. She is very orderly, pretty much black and white, so I wanted to be sure her page reflected her likes. I did the same of Clairity. Her page would be all the colors in a rainbow, it reminded me of a full spectrum color-wheel.

I wanted my page to reflect the center, a new woman with a new inspired outlook on life. In-spirit and inspired. I chose white and gold for my page.

Once I started to assemble the "weave" I noticed Nora's part didn't seem to reflect her as much as she'd like. So instead of handwriting the words on Nora's page I typed them on my computer and printed it out. When I used the printed page, I felt much better about it. This was definitely more Nora's style—very neat!

I joined the water-soaked paint brush with the rainbow paints and dropped them on Clairity's page. I noticed some of the words that had been written became smeared, some un-legible. I liked the effect as it looked artsy to me.

I continued and cut the Saboteur and Muse's pages into ¼" strips. I took the strips in random order I started weaving them between the strips of my page. I randomly selected which strip was woven next until there were no more. I tacked the sides and bottom of the weave. I took the finished weave and grabbed both sides and intuitively pulled! Then I turned it and pulled the opposite ... even diagonally ... it was strong! It wouldn't tear or rip.

This was a representation of the new me. The confident me. The strong me. The passionate me. The clearheaded me. The prosperous me. The manifesting me. The reconciled me. Reconciled? I hadn't felt this way for as long as I can remember, probably because I had never been reconciled like this before. Previously, reconciliation was between me and another person, or a religious entity. "I've been forgiven sort of thing." But this time this was different. How could I really have felt forgiven or reconciled when deep down I had the inner critic inside telling me otherwise? This had to come first.

The Weave had to come first.

It felt complete and I felt whole, probably for the first time in my life.

"The Weave"

15
Role Playing

*Empathize and gain insight by stepping
inside for a different perspective.*

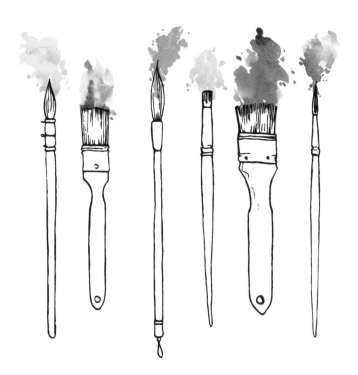

After I'd finished with the actual Weave, I talked with my friend Meridian and shared the full project I'd done with her. She was intrigued and excited to go through the process, because she could see the difference it had made in me. After walking her through what I'd been given, she told me how much she loved it and could see how this could be wonderful to share with others.

Shortly afterwards, Meridian was happy to tell me her Saboteur's name was Sara Rose. The two of us met up for an afternoon together and I had the idea that we should role play as if we were our Saboteurs, just for the fun of it. My thought behind this was the more we understood our Saboteurs, the more we'd understand ourselves. This would give us more power!

We decided to go out shopping and lunch like we'd done many times before, but this time we were role playing as if we were our Saboteurs, Nora and Sara Rose. It felt like we were both kids again playing make believe. We focused on the personalities and profiles of each of our Saboteurs and we already knew we were going to have fun role playing.

As we were walking on the sidewalk, a shop window display caught Nora's eye, so we both went in. To my surprise and to Nora's delight, the entire store was filled with taupe and navy clothing and a splash white (which I like). Even the carpet was taupe color. Nora quickly went to the women's racks, lightly moving her fingers across the hanger tops, feeling the fabric and observing the quality of which they were made. She was in heaven as both Navy and Taupe were two of the colors I refused to wear. I didn't like either one of them and there were no traces of these colors in my closet. I would have never considered going into this shop before. Even though it was in my neighborhood, I found it interesting that I'd never seen this store before. After several minutes, Nora was ready to move on, she was happy that she'd been validated.

We went to several stores, looking for the items our Saboteurs would like and of course what they didn't like. I noticed Sara Rose was attracted to party dresses, some a bit wild. At one point, Sara Rose asked Nora what she thought of the dress she was holding. Nora's immediate response was to say "whore"! We both broke out in laughter! We had so much fun as we took turns being overly dramatic playing our new roles.

At some point we unanimously decided to get something to eat and drink. We found a place just around the corner, which was good, because Nora certainly does not like the Florida heat. We walked inside and saw the restaurant was full, so we made our way to the bar where we saw two available seats. When the bartender asked what I wanted to drink, as if I was possessed, the words, "I'll have a gin gimlet" jumped out of my mouth. I was shocked because I had no idea what I'd just ordered, but Nora knew exactly what she was doing apparently. Meridian ordered a soda which surprised me because I was sure she'd order her usual, or at least a glass of wine. My drink arrived and I took my first sip ever of this perfect looking martini with a lime slice. I was amused at how much I liked it especially since I didn't like gin and it was strong. The hint of sweet lime juice was ever so refreshing. Besides, I had to agree with Nora's fondness of how the martini glass looks.

That afternoon was pivotal in that this was truly the day I fell in love with Nora. The role playing was fun yet insightful. I found I had compassion for Nora, just like we would anyone else we get to know intimately. She was clearly afraid and the longer she was in charge the more afraid she became. So now I've taken the burden off of Nora so she can do what's she's good at. She can take a break from the burden of thinking she had to take care of me. I know that she wanted the best for me, but she was misguided and uninformed.

16
Where is Sara Rose?

Playing Hide and Seek

A few weeks later I drove down to Sarasota to visit Meridian, because we wanted to discuss holding a Saboteur-Muse workshop for a group of businesswomen in Sarasota. We sat down at her kitchen table, chatting over a cup of tea and looking at our notes. It had occurred to me that I hadn't seen her Saboteur. "Show me your Saboteur," I said. Meridian pulled out her notes, had all the descriptions, and some drawings, but she couldn't find it. We both scoured her place trying to find where she might have put her saboteur. She finally came up with a drawing, but it was of a flowery tablecloth with a teacup & saucer, a tea pot, but nowhere was Sara Rose. It felt like she was playing hide and seek. Meridian surmised she'd not actually drawn her.

I found it such an important element of the download that I just couldn't let her go without putting Sara Rose on paper. She needed to know what she looked like. It was a key element of the project to healing our hurt selves. I didn't want to push her at the moment so we went ahead and talked about when we could hold the workshop. Later that afternoon we went out for lunch, then headed to the beach to get some sun baking and swimming in before I headed back up to Sarasota. As soon as we got comfortable on our lounge chairs, I took out my pen and notebook, turned it to a blank page and handed them to Meridian saying, "You've got 3 minutes to draw Sara Rose ... GO!"

I watched as Meridian quickly brought Sara Rose to life on the beach. I was surprised at what I saw, and Meridian looked even more surprised. She sat there looking stunned, saying nothing for several minutes. Then she said to me, "This explains everything. My life has been run by a five-year-old, a scared five-year-old. No wonder."

Sara Rose couldn't look at you from the sheet of paper she was on. Her head was looking sideways, a profile. She looked like an afraid child and with pursed lips. There was something endearing about her. Of course, this explained why Sara Rose ordered a soda the other day when we were role playing. Sara Rose was trying to tell my friend she was really just a little girl. A five-year old girl with a big responsibility!

"Sara Rose"

17
Race Day Trophy

The word trophy was derived from
the French trophee:
"a prize of war."

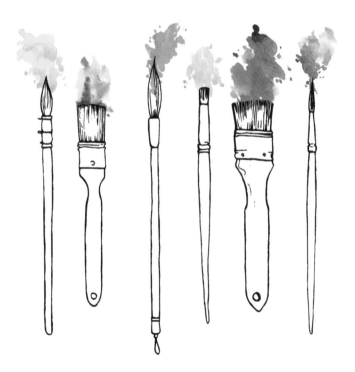

The day before race day, I decided to circle back to my Muse. I felt amazing, strong, and even beautiful. My Muse was a beautiful part of me. Clairity was my Divine spirit guide, she knew I could do whatever I wanted to do. She knew I would be safe, and I knew she believed in happily ever after. It wasn't a fairy-tale. It could be my life if I decided to place my focus on what I desired and was appreciative of my life every day. My comfort zone was expanding now that my Saboteur was no longer keeping me from living the life I wanted to live. I had a strong feeling that I could have what I wanted, and most importantly I felt worthy of my dreams.

I spent several hours of the day visualizing running tomorrow's race, crossing the finish line and feeling enthusiastic and watching the people cheering me on. I was ready! We were ready to do this: Me, Nora and Clairity!

Race day. In the past there would have been a high likelihood of me not showing up for the race. My excuses would be:

- I signed up for the 10k by accident.

- It was too hot.

- The humidity was unbearable.

- I'm too old.

- No one cares whether I run the race or not.

- Social media friends would soon forget and stop cheering for me.

- I had no one to run with me.

- I'm not a runner, who am I kidding?

- No one will hold me accountable.

- I could get heat stroke.

- I'll embarrass myself.

Normally, I only needed one of these excuses not to follow through with it.

However, this day was different, because of what I heard the day I was running along Tampa's bay. I clearly heard both the Saboteur and the Muse. I couldn't get around it and intuitively I knew this was something special and most of all, it was important to me moving forward. Because I heard what I heard, I wanted to keep running in case I heard either one of them shouting at me. Running became my meditation time, and creative thinking outside the box time.

The race was being held in Saint Petersburg, FL on a Saturday in the morning. There was a big crowd of people, maybe not as big as the event in San Francisco, but because it is so flat in Florida, there really wasn't any place for me to get an overall view of the event like I could have in the prior location. Having said that, I really had no idea of how it compared to San Fran's numbers.

I made my way to the booth to sign in, picked up my runner's number, and waited for my turn to start the race. I'd calculated the time I thought I could run the 10K (6.3miles) based on my running route near my apartment. I was a bit nervous waiting my turn. I hadn't run this route before, but there were signs posted along the way, so I knew I probably wouldn't get lost and my husband would know where to look for me if I happened to collapse on my way around the course. It was going to be another hot humid day, although I was thankful there was a cloud cover which was a blessing as far as I was concerned. I was filling up with water so I wouldn't get dehydrated and stretching my legs as I heard my group being called to get ready.

"On your mark, get set ... GO!" The street was crowded with runners, shoulder to shoulder. I couldn't see anyone on the sidelines, only the narrow focal point ahead of me all with wearing numbers on their backs.

Once I had a little room around me. I became aware of my breathing and consciously focused on my breathing in ... and breathing out ... in a rhythm ... my rhythm.

As I turned the corner heading into a different direction away from the big buildings of the city center, I wasn't prepared for the long stretch of road I saw ahead. The road had an incline. Shit! I hadn't expected this! Sure it wasn't what I'd normally call a hill, but in Florida, I definitely felt this would have been considered a hill. It was a long road as far as I could see, maybe 3 miles, and I noticed I was running mostly by myself. The runner's must have spread themselves out running their pace. I was thinking I had fallen behind a bit because of the darned hill; no one was around me.

I had a wave of loneliness sweep over me. Then I remembered I wasn't alone. I had brought Nora and Clairity with me, and I was reminded I was still running. I wasn't ready to give up just yet. Noticeably, Nora was silent.

Breathing In ...

One ... two ... three ... whhh ... whhh ... whhh

Breathing Out ...

One ... two ... three ... shhh ... shhh ... shhh ...

Breathing In ...

One ... two ... three ... whhh ... whhh ... whhh ...

Breathing Out ...

One ... two ... three ... shhh ... shhh ... shhh ...

Over and over again until I reached the state of mind where I no longer needed to focus on my breath, only my thoughts and watching my steps one after another. Again, I noticed no other runners around me. I was thinking I must have fallen way behind but was still determined to keep going as my legs and lungs were still working. I found myself thinking of the new scenery, the city's downtown buildings and the Weave Project. How different I felt just a short month ago.

I felt emotionally strong, probably for the first time in my life. No, it's definitely for the first time in my life adult life. My mind was thinking of this very moment, and what I was actually doing. My first "official" running a race. I still wasn't sure whether I was going to be able to finish it running or walking across the finish line, but I'd have at least given it my best and my best is good enough. It felt great! I wasn't out to beat the other runners. I was however out to beat myself from not stopping the race.

There was a directional sign up ahead and I felt somewhat of a relief that I'd made it up the hill without stopping or walking. I turned the corner and all the sudden there was a crowd of runners all around me. I kicked up my pace a bit. I was feeling really good and surprising myself that I still felt strong as the salty sweat was running down my face. My hair was soaked beneath my hat, and my entire body was glistening. I knew I had the strength to finish.

The other runners were also speeding up. I had to focus on my breathing again, but this time it was different. I was already in what I'd call an altered mental state and it seemed as if I was looking down at myself running. I was watching myself run shoulder to shoulder with the other runners, visualizing myself crossing the finish line with people cheering for me. I was thinking of spending time with the people in my life that I love and freely feeling it.

I was awakened from my runner's trance as I turned the last corner. I could see the finish line banner stretched across the road. I couldn't feel my legs, but I knew they were still working. I gave it my one last push to speed up and passed a few people. As soon as I crossed the finish line, I stopped running but was still walking, slowly becoming aware of my body again. I was overwhelmed emotionally and burst into tears. This race was so much more than a race for me; it changed me.

When I saw my finish time on the clock at 01.13 hours (8.4-minute miles). I was a bit in shock and amazed that I'd come in a good 20+ minutes before I thought I would. That explained why I was running alone much of the time. I'd left the group I'd started with behind and ended up catching up with the group ahead of me.

I felt proud of myself. Nothing or no one could take this from me. I felt confident going forward in making new plans for my life and my freedom. Both Nora and Clairity were on my side, and Nora knew I would need her help in getting me organized. I could feel that Clairity had new adventures, challenges and joy ahead for us.

The Long Stretch

Crossing the Finish Line

Feeling Amazing

18

Taking a Seat with My Muse

I imagine sitting beside my Muse becoming connected to my Divine guide.

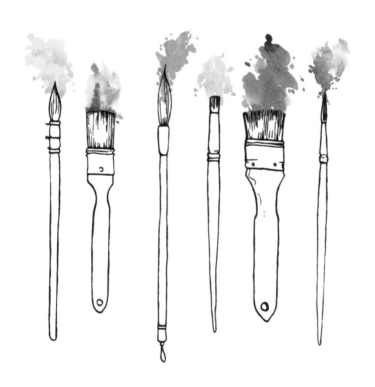

To be honest, I wasn't used to listening for or hearing from Clairity. Over the years I'd grown a solid habit of listening to the self-talk of my Saboteur and I'd had a tendency to focus on the negative self-talk whenever I heard it. I started wondering why we humans so easily focus on the negative versus the positive. The negative certainly doesn't make me, or anyone else I know, feel good that's for sure. It did give me an excuse not to step out of my comfort zone to follow my dreams. I'm being very transparent in saying it took me some time—longer than I'd wanted—to create new mindset habits. I knew I needed to create new habits because I wanted this to be a permanent change, not a short lived "event" in my life.

Although, because of the details and steps of calling out my Saboteur and giving Nora a job, I did feel I'd done a pretty thorough job of making sure that part of myself was put to bed so to speak. Yet I was listening, watching and on guard for any signs of them rearing their head back into mine. I'm very glad and relieved to say that my Saboteur has not become active again (with the rare exception when I call on her for help with her given job). Sure, I might question certain things that may have come my way, but it wasn't in a negative way. It was more of me investigating, then making a decision one way or another.

I wanted this new life I'd been given a glimpse of; this new me, which included my muse, Clairity, being by my side. I knew in my heart the Muse was an important part of the project that I was presented and couldn't be put aside. Clairity was my future. I wanted to dive deeper with this new-to-me, part of me. I became hungry to know more and hungry for a new life. I felt if I kept putting one foot in front of the other, I'd finally get out of the "living in the in-between" situation I'd gotten myself stuck in for the past several years.

I felt Clairity was my Divine spirit guide, offering those quiet or not so quiet soul nudges attached directly to my intuition. I've felt those nudges on many occasions in the past, but more often than not, I chose not to listen, mostly because the Saboteur would convince me otherwise. Instead I heard "Play it safe" vs "Let's play, adventure, and spread your wings, Darla." So I decided it was in my best interest to take a seat with Clairity on a regular basis. At first, I kept her picture open so I could see her. I love her picture, mostly because of what it represents to me and how it makes me feel. Which was and is ALIVE!

I'd been wanting to meditate and had been promising myself I was going start a regular meditation practice for a long time, but was never able to keep the promise to myself. I'd read quite a bit of magazine articles, books and other expert's writings on the benefits of meditation when practiced regularly. I felt meditation was not only something I needed, but I wanted to do. Meditating was a healthy way to help calm my nerves, to become happy and at peace. I wanted to be consistent in becoming more aware of my mental states, and to learn to differentiate between the normal everyday intuitive thoughts and hearing from Clairity. I purposely invited Clairity into my meditation practices. As I did, I imagined sitting down next to my Muse, taking a seat beside her, and becoming connected to the Divine guide.

This was what I wanted in my life every day ... all day, not just moments of it. Yes, I needed this too.

I was a bit surprised, but once I decided with conviction that I'd begin my meditation practice and make it a part of my daily life, I found it was easier than I'd thought it would be. In the past when I'd attempted to practice meditation, the voice of my Saboteur would always get involved. Before I knew it, I was doing something else other than meditating like focusing on some problem. But now, this time, I found I didn't hear the distractions (at least not nearly as often) and I was finally able to place my focus of just "noticing" vs entertaining a rampage of thoughts that had nothing to do with my desire to meditate.

I started out creating the habit of meditation by practicing placing my focus on my Muse—in a high regard to her. Trying to just notice how I was feeling. I noticed how my body felt, and tried to notice without my "thoughts." I was just BEING ... being with Clairity.

I'd noticed objects in the room, purposely without having judgement or thoughts. When I'd find myself "thinking" again, I'd simply go back to noticing. I'd read somewhere to not be judgmental or hard on myself when my habitual busy mind started to wander off. As soon as I noticed I was "in a stream of thoughts," I'd be kind to myself and simply readjust back to the "no thoughts of just Being." I'd notice the weave of the fabric that I'd wrapped myself in or notice the colors I saw when I closed my eyes. It felt so good to me. I could feel the vibration of my body, usually starting with my hands and then through-out my body. I'm pretty sure it was the energy I was getting by putting myself, and my mind, in a sacred space.

I found it worked best for me when I have quiet background noise I could notice, either a sound of the cooling system, or a nonverbal tone such as a lingering bell sound. I'd found on an App for my phone that I use pretty much every day that helps me keep track of my meditation time. I vary how I keep track, but usually I stick to the one that works best for me and Clairity.

I started to dream again. I started remembering the things that inspired me. Remembering the places I'd wanted to visit or live. Taking in the feelings of being able to do it and not the how of it. I was relishing in the feelings of loving my life whether it had manifested my dream to me already or was waiting patiently for me to claim it.

Taking a seat with my Muse is sacred to me. I feel the love and I adore it. Today I meditate almost daily in the mornings. It has helped me to stay focused on what is real, how truly wonderful my life has been unfolding, and how much I have to appreciate!

19
A Second Saboteur

It's not finished until the fat lady sings.

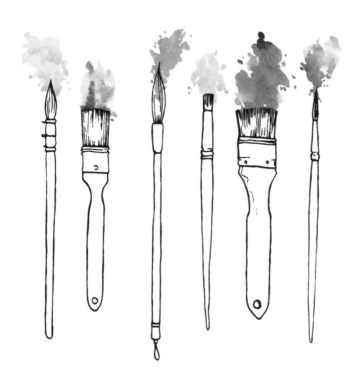

Several months after I'd finished the Weave, I noticed I was having some minor negative self-talk. Although it was negative, this time it was different. It was nothing like my Saboteur Nora. It was almost like the opposite of Nora, but a saboteur none the less. It obviously wasn't anything like my Muse Clairity either.

I found myself having some shoulds and shouldn'ts, coming into my mind. I knew it wasn't Nora because the words should and shouldn't weren't a part of Nora's normal vocabulary. Once I noticed this, I knew I needed to address it before it got out of control and landed in my subconscious mindset. I decided I'd better take myself through the first part of the project again, primarily just the part of calling out a Saboteur.

I was living back in Oregon and was feeling I'd made huge progress in moving forward with my life. I had to take care of pretty much everything because I was on my own. I thought I was capable of doing everything that came my way, yet I had this nagging feeling that I was still living in the in-between. I wasn't divorced yet; we were separated, and I knew I wasn't in a marriage that felt like what a relationship should be, let alone what a marriage should be. I was definitely well into middle-age and pushing the boundaries of not being on the youthful side of life.

I was busy. As soon as I returned home, I hit the road running. I was busy working my vacation rental business as it was the beginning of the summer season. I'd also started networking and expanding my circle of friends and influence. I was keeping up my home, learning how to be a "handy-woman," paying bills, doing what I could to keep my head above water. I had a growing business but still felt I had more to do to "make it." I knew I was spreading myself thin and sometimes it felt like I was walking a tightrope. The negative voice definitely wasn't as strong as Nora's was, but something or someone was there, and I knew I had to nip it in the bud quickly. I'd been studying how the mind works, as I was thirsty to know more about the why of dysfunctional and abusive personalities (primarily for my own self- preservation).

It was early in the morning; the cool air had filled my bedroom overnight and I could smell the coffee floating up the stairs. I pulled myself out of bed. I made my way down to pour myself a hot mug full to the brim. Today was the day I was going to meet this part of me, this "new" Saboteur.

I went to my favorite spot in the house, upstairs in the nook I'd had built several years earlier. It was a little bit of heaven there for me—cozy, comfy, and safe feeling with just the right amount of light filtering in from the windows that overlooked the wisteria covered pergola. The sheer white curtains hanging in front of the entrance were moving slightly with the breeze. I had my grandmother's handmade quilt wrapped around me as I sat with my laptop and the large notebook/artbook where the original Saboteur and Muse came to life. I opened the book, moving past the original project where Nora and Clairity emerged, and stopped until I came upon some blank pages. I waited ... staring at the blank pages; listening to what I'd had been telling myself, until the words fell on to the page.

"I'm smarter than everyone else. Just don't do it. Who cares anyway? You shouldn't do this. This is below you. This isn't what you need to do. Stay on the couch and watch movies with me. You know you want to. Screw your diet—get the ice cream and eat it—all of it! You know you want to and you know you should. Who cares anyway? Eat whatever you feel like. Stay home. Don't answer the door. Don't answer the phone. Don't look at your emails. You're better off being alone. Besides, anything you need can be delivered to the door. Don't take a shower today; don't wash your face; no one is going to see you anyway; No one cares. Don't wash your hair; it's too bothersome. You should stop and be smart like me. Be comfortable and wear a muu muu! Oh and by the way, you should never date, period."

Whoa!! What the heck? I was feeling confused to say the least. This saboteur was so different than Nora, yet I knew she was sabotaging me from doing what I wanted and especially what I thought I needed to do.

I decided I wanted to see her. I needed to see her. So I took a pencil and placed it on her page. I just let the pencil take the lead ... kind of like I was just feeling her instead of trying to analyze.

As I drew her, this Saboteur was sloppy, and a big girl, a really big girl. Her hair was mousy brown just below her shoulders and it was greasy (from lack of washing or combing it). Her skin was bad, not clear. She had brown eyes and was wearing glasses. She was wearing a lightweight dress, not fitted in any manner. It reminded me of something my maternal grandmother would have worn: mid-calf, with a pattern of tiny flowers, kind of muted, certainly not bright. She had a stain on the front of the dress, which must have been from some food. She was holding in one of her hands a partially eaten chocolate candy bar with the wrapper torn down.

Her favorite things were ice cream, chocolate and sandwiches made with chewie sourdough sliced bread.

She only likes to wear dresses, of a thin fabric (so she doesn't get hot) with tiny flowers. Her favorite colors are tan and light blue, sometimes green and lavender. Most of her dresses came from thrift stores like the Goodwill that even when new, probably cost no more than $25.00 ever.

She peeks outside the windows so no one will see her. She never goes outside, and says if humans were meant to be outside, we'd have fur all over our bodies for protection.

She reads every day, usually history and scientific journals. She can't stand fiction or self-help books. She does love to watch tv, documentaries, foreign films with subtitles, an occasional romantic comedy, antique road show, drama series and police shows.

The thing was, after finding out what she likes and what she doesn't like, and what she looks like, I wasn't able to pinpoint what she was good at just yet. She seemed to only be exceptional at being critical of everyone else. I decided to just stop the process, take a break, wait and revisit her. Besides I had work to do. I honestly think the thing driving me to know her was that I was feeling like I was living in the in-between ... stuck between not really living fully, and just going through the motions. I was still haunted by the feeling like I wasn't really living the life I wanted. In fairness, I didn't even really know what it was I wanted.

I knew my Muse was there for me, but she wasn't someone I was accessing regularly. I'd gotten so involved with being busy and doing all the things I thought I needed to do to survive on my own. Little did I know that I needed my Muse, now more than ever.

That evening after I'd taken care of my business for the day, I poured myself a healthy glass of pinot noir, tore off a hunk of yesterday's loaf of bread, grabbed a string cheese in its tidy packet (after I checked the use by date, which was barely over a week) and made my way up the stairs, noticing how heavy my legs felt. I dropped my clothes on the floor and pulled on my comfy pjs. I finally settled back in the nook, again wrapping myself in my grandmother's quilt.

I purposefully looked at the words on her page with the eye of Headhunter looking for the perfect job for her. I was tired from the day but was trying to wind down and relax, so I'd be open to whatever this saboteur had to offer. Then it suddenly hit me, without evaluating anything. She's really good at putting herself first, and doing what she feels like, with no apologies. Her job, when I need it, was to be ok about taking a break: Self-care.

Before I closed this saboteur's page, I needed to do one last thing: Give her a name. Thinking about how outrageous she was, the name Lola slipped into my mind. No need to look any further. Lola it was, and I think it made both of us happy.

I don't know why this was such a big deal for me but apparently, I'm not super woman, or the I-can-do-everything-every-time kind of woman. Lola provided permission to be the break I needed. This break gave me time to sit back and evaluate what I wanted, and most importantly time to get reconnected with Clairity, my muse.

"Lola"

20
Minding My Mindset

Your mindset can be changed and that changes your life.

It wasn't long after the Weave was over that I'd started questioning, or should I say, I continued questioning just about everything. Through the Weave process I realized our minds were more powerful than I knew, the more I questioned and dove into the depths of how and why of my thoughts and how others think. There was a pattern I began noticing in those people who were familiar to me. This was what led me to my profession today.

In my prior work I'd found myself in banking management, as a law firm administrator and then made the jump into self-employment. I got into real estate as an investor and property management which also morphed into the new short-term vacation rentals. I even worked in the yachting industry as a co-inventor of a product for small boats and super yachts. All this experience helped me to learn how to be successfully self-employed, in business practices, strategies and structures. Because of the Weave, I decided to change the course I was on as an entrepreneur. I became passionate about doing what I wanted to do.

I discovered, or a better term would be, "awakened" to the fact I'd been surrounding myself around various forms of abusive people. It took a counselor to ask me a life awakening question, which actually made me mad when he asked me. "Why is it acceptable for you to be abused?"

I felt instantly defensive and replied with an almost sarcastic tone, "I don't accept it. This is the reason I'm here in your office!"

He responded, "YES IT IS! No other healthy woman would accept this. You've been doing this for years, so it IS acceptable to you!" He asked me again, "So why is it acceptable to you?"

I sat there in shock. Once I settled down, I could feel the nudge of truth wanting to come to the surface. A truth that I'd held a secret deep inside. I did not want to accept this as my truth. I am not a victim and I wanted my childhood memories to be perfect.

Which, as the truth finally bubbled up, they weren't. Growing up my mother was hard on me ... very hard, bordering on abuse at times. My brother was a big mean bully and physically abusive to me as well. I'd become an expert at hiding behind my smile and fooled myself for many years. I was living in denial. I knew I needed to break away from my husband. But I was scared. Scared of him, yes, but also scared to break out on my own. I'd been married for the majority of my adult life. I'd never really been alone for very long, so I put up with behaviors that would not be acceptable to most people. I realized I was part of the problem as well, so I'm not pointing any fingers. I won't go into the details of what happened, but I knew I had to get away or I would end up dying, if not physically, then certainly, emotionally and spiritually. I'd been diagnosed with PTSD, insomnia, blown adrenals and low thyroid disease by my physician.

I honestly believe the Weave saved me. It enabled me to take a good hard look at myself and my self-talk. It enabled me to grow up and accept responsibility for myself. It gave me huge insights about how our mind works and how to create a life of happiness, joy and love. Most importantly it taught me how to find and attain Self-love. It taught me how to not only love myself fully but how to love others as well, because we really can't love others when we're not able to love ourselves. When we don't love ourselves, our perception of love is different than when we are able to love ourselves. Part of self-love is not allowing others to bully or abuse me. I am done with that; the old beliefs, the dysfunctional behaviors and the acceptance of them.

The farther I am from the day I heard the words from my Saboteur when I was running on the Bay, the closer I get to living my dream life every single day.

I began studying the mind. I read everything I could get my hands on that led me further into the workings and behaviors of our mindsets. I was hungry to find out why we do what we do and most importantly how to change what isn't working in our favor for the long haul. I say this because often short-term gains can be alluring, but they end up just being band-aids.

I started with Neuro-Linguistic Programing, most often referred to as NLP, basically Neuro (Mind), Linguistics (Language) Programing (Pattern). From there I studied Hypnosis which I found to be most helpful and interesting. I felt like I'd just hit the gussying oil well. Here I learned how to change the old mindset patterns that no longer work for me. I learned how powerful humans are. I believe most have the power to change their lives when they change their mind patterns, aka habits.

I also studied a lesser known, yet very powerful mindset reset process called TimeLine Therapy™. This was what I'd been waiting for. This process can take all our limiting beliefs about ourselves and negative emotions and change how we think about them, giving us a new perspective. Once we have a different perspective of something, we can have a new outlook, a new opinion and a new direction. The reason TimeLine Therapy™ is so powerful, even over standard Hypnotherapy, is that the person undergoing the process receives their own answers, from their higher Divine Source, versus hearing it from an outside person. In hypnosis generally, the Hypnotherapist gives the patient suggestions while they are in a trance-like mental state.

I became very aware of how I was feeling both emotionally and physically. I became in tune to my vibes. I made myself number one. Some people may have issues with this. But honestly if you don't put your emotional wellbeing first, how can you fully be there for others? If you think you can, well, I'd be willing to bet the love for others is probably skewed in some manner or another.

I noticed when I had fears or other negative emotions come up, my body seemed to react before I actually had the thought of fear. This was because of the "fight or flight" reactions, or our mindset wiring that we all have. Because of the Weave, I became very aware of what was happening physically and emotionally in myself. I made it my top priority to be in a state of mind that was, peaceful, happy, calm, clear, joyful, creative, at ease, feeling abundant, etc. This became my daily monitor of how I was doing. I knew my Muse was always present with me and knowing this made it easier to stay grounded. I used whatever tools I could find to help me stay on track. It was easier not having the negative self-talk pattern any longer, but I had other habits that were keeping my dream life just out of reach.

I wanted it all. If I was truthful with myself, I didn't want to settle. My Muse didn't want me to settle either. I learned that my old lifelong mindset patterns could be changed and yes there was something I could do about it. But I also knew that it takes a vision of what you want to have enough pull for you to get it. When you use what you don't want to make changes in your life, it is harder to make those changes stick. I've learned that you've got to have a good idea of what you want; you need to ((feel)) it in your body as if it is already done.

Having feelings, good emotions and a mindset that works for you is key by placing your focus on the positive and what you want.

- Feeling peaceful

- Being happy

- Feeling calm

- Being joyful

- Feeling creative

- Being at ease

- Feeling clear

- Being free flowing

- Feeling love

- Being confident

- Feeling prosperous

Ignore everything else. No need to focus on the states of mind that works against you, that just reaffirms the negative.

21
Outside Influences
(SABOTEURS OUTSIDE OURSELVES)

*Just when you thought it
was safe to go in the water.*

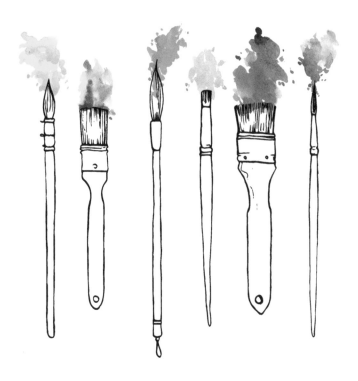

Again, being honest with myself, I had to accept the fact that I'd been self-sabotaging myself for years. It was no one else's fault. I am the only one that is responsible for my life.

Acknowledging this fact was a big one for me. I had no one else to blame. I no longer needed to blame anyone else. The Weave set me up to be honest with myself, vulnerable and willing to grow through personal development.

I now knew my worth and I found the perfect love. It was inside of me!

Yet, there are some people, outside of the self, that have big personalities, big anger, and big issues themselves. They can feel the need validate and protect their ego and will often try to overpower others who seem weaker than themselves. Even as an adult I was easily manipulated and controlled because of the outbursts of anger that turned into an "I'm-so-sorry-merry-go-round" that's very hard to get off. I was afraid and rightfully so. Outside saboteurs can be dangerous, abusive and a real threat—not just a perceived one. My inner saboteur fed right into it. This is where "living in the in-between" took its strong foothold on me. As I alluded to earlier in the book, my second marriage was full of challenges. It was nothing less than dysfunctional and very unhealthy. It not only affected me but was unhealthy for my precious daughter and other close family members. My inability to get out of this relationship kept me living in the in-between. I was frozen. Frozen from the "what if?" scenarios that were filled with fear. It felt like what I imagine as being the yoyo at the end of the string. It was a relationship of highs and then out of nowhere ... abrupt lows, fits of rage, and huge remorse.

The truth is, once you know who you really are, not who your inner Saboteur says you are, and treat yourself with kindness and love, there isn't anything you can't do that you truly want to do.

I changed my mind. I changed my behavior, which changed my emotions, and I changed the vision of my future.

I knew I was no longer going to stay stuck. Saboteurs outside ourselves, especially those who are in our inner circle may not like the new you. Most people don't like change. I had to be very careful in separating myself from my main outside Saboteur and I knew it would take time. But I felt strong, and I had new a life I wanted to live that was free from those outside influences.

There are also more subtle saboteurs that can often be given authority (by you) to derail your plans. Some of the most caring, loving people in your life can unknowingly try to stop you from living out your dreams. They just see things from their perspective. They do it because they don't want to see you fail, or to be disappointed. They just don't think you have what it takes to do the things you want to do, or are sure that you don't really know what you are getting yourself into. They may believe they know better than you do. They may not yet have the experience needed to be in a profession that has influence on others, especially children.

Saboteurs outside of ourselves can also come from social media, news media, governments, religious leaders, bosses, co-workers, friends, even misinformed professionals i.e., so called business experts in legal, health, medical, pharmaceuticals and the list can go on and on.

Take the lead from The Weave and identify those parts of you that are not working in your favor, the ones that keep you stuck or in the "I'm not good enough" mode of life. Employing the steps I received made it much easier to know where my limiting and negative thoughts came from. It allowed me to get to the root cause.

The root cause is a term that's often used in hypnotherapy and other therapies. The first occurrence of a negative event that has happened is the Root Cause. In my case, my fear of talking in front of more than 3 people at a time came from the root cause when I gave my book report as a child. Once the root cause is determined, it can be dealt with and more often than not, gives the person a new perspective. Having a different perspective of a negative event is often the catalyst for turning things around for people.

- You may find the negative event wasn't about you at all.

- You may find the negative event wasn't your fault.

- You may find the negative event wasn't worthy of ruining your life.

- You may find the negative event is worthy of forgiveness.

- You may find your feeling about the negative event isn't worth holding on to.

In most cases this is what I've found to be true when working with clients.

Taking the next steps from The Weave can also give you tools to move forward. Developing your Muse by taking care of your inner spirit creates safety. Letting go of the negative self-talk and the associated physical emotions they create in the body and grabbing on to the hand of your Muse is key for your future. You're not left on your own, you're left with the Divine by your side.

Breathe In ... Love.

Breath Out ... Forgiveness.

Breathe In ... Joy.

Breathe Out ... Ease.

22

I Changed My Mind ...
It Changed My Life

We are born creators
and the adventurers of life.

After the Weave, my life took many good turns, and I eventually ended up at where I am today.

Today ... I have clarity of mind.

Today ... I am confident.

Today ... I am prosperous.

Today ... I am happy.

Today ... I love myself.

Today... I have no regrets (only lessons).

Today... I am following my Joy.

The fact is, when I dove deep into getting to know why I kept sabotaging myself and then being able to change, it changed my perspective. The Weave helped me to separate my unhealthy thoughts, limiting beliefs, and the habitual negative emotions in my body from who I really am. It gave me the opportunity to have compassion for myself, to be easy on myself and extend that to others as well.

I was able to get in touch with my inner guide, my Muse. I learned to take the time I needed to develop a strong relationship with the Divine part of me. My life has continued to unfold in ways that I'd couldn't have even imagined before the Weave.

I took a leap of faith and enrolled in school receiving my Master certifications in Hypnotherapy, NLP (Neuro-Linguistic Programming), Life Coaching and TimeLine Therapy™. I started my own business as a Lifestyle Architect helping women gain clarity, confidence and prosperity. I felt confident knowing the Weave was completely in line with the education I received and was easily able to integrate it into my practice. I developed the

Saboteur-Muse Project™ for women's creativity retreats. Since then, it's become the signature program for my Coaching Practice and have found it to be a highly valuable process in all areas of life for women. It helps them to shed the misconceptions of who they are, and what they can do.

On a more personal note, I was brave enough to follow my Muse, followed the advice of my doctors and safely divorced my husband. The fears I had previously were gone and I was comfortable on my own with very little financial support from my Ex or anyone else.

I founded a women's networking group in Southern Oregon called the Rogue Moxies, helping women with business strategies and lifestyle. Together we created a close-knit sisterhood community that supports and encourages one another.

I was finally truly happy with my life and was happy with myself. I was helping women in my community, and my practice of hypnotherapy and life coaching was doing well and supporting my lifestyle. I was feeling that life was pretty darned good. I liked being single and after dating a couple of men, I decided I was completely okay being by myself. I no longer felt the need to be rescued and I wasn't about to settle. I knew the only person I needed in my life to have a fulfilling life was me. My life was full and good.

A year or so later, when I was meditating in my favorite spot in the house (in the cozy nook), I was paying attention to the energy in my body, by quieting my mind, taking deep slow breaths with my main intention of discovering clarity. This particular day was different as a vision came to me. It was so clear, almost as if I'd been transported into it. I was in an art gallery. The gallery was fairly narrow but deep, maybe 40 to 50 feet long. There was beautiful art on the walls and near the back of the gallery was my desk, my dog curled up in her bed. The entire back wall was a waterfall wall. The soothing sound of the water gently rolling down could be heard once stepping into the gallery space. In the center of the gallery was a tall simple stand with a beautiful orchid perched on top with a light from high above shining down on it. The Orchid seemed to glow.

The feeling of this vision was so real and lifelike. It felt so good. I had a sense of ease, lightness and happiness. A handsome middle-aged man walked into the gallery, holding a folded newspaper in one of his hands. He was casually dressed but looked put together. He was similar height to me, with salt and pepper hair. In my vision, I knew him. We were together, a couple, and he'd just stopped by to say hello. The very next scene, the two of us were in a beautiful condo preparing dinner together in the kitchen. We were having fun, sharing tasks in preparing the meal; it was completely easy and comfortable. The next scene we were sitting at the long narrow dining table with several good friends, laughing, eating, and enjoying good wine.

Then "poof" my vision was gone.

I've lost count of how many times I'd go back to that vision. It was so real. The feeling I had whenever I went back to it was always the same. It felt really good; I felt good, and I felt it was real. That's all I needed ... my vision was enough.

I didn't long for the mystery man, but I did have a sense of knowing.

A couple years later, a new member of the women's networking group asked if I'd consider dating. My answer to her was, "Well, it depends." She went on to tell me that she knew my good energy and she knew his energy and thought we'd make a good match.

He and I exchanged some emails and had some fairly unsuccessful phone calls because I had a hard time understanding him on the phone. He spoke English but he had an accent.

We finally arranged to meet. We didn't live in the same town, or state. For that matter, he was from a different country all together—Australia. I was beginning to wonder what my friend was thinking. But then again, I thought what could it hurt? It would be refreshing to meet someone who didn't live in my small hometown.

At seven o'clock on the dot, I heard a knock on the door. "Prompt ... that's nice." We had a lovely date. He was a gentleman, opening the doors, and taking me to my favorite restaurant for dinner and drinks. He had a great sense of humor and easily made me laugh, which I hadn't done with a man in a very long time. Afterwards we went back to my place to talk a bit more. He was easy to understand in person, it was just on the phone I had trouble hearing his pronunciations.

At some point in the evening we both had the feeling that we'd known each other but had no idea why. All I knew at the time, was that it was comfortable.

We continued to date, traveling to So. California and back and forth to Australia and Oregon. We became best friends and have been practically inseparable. It was and continues to be an adventure with him. We ended up getting married 5½ years after we were first introduced. Our relationship is the best either one of us has had, and neither one of us had thought we'd ever get married again.

Today, I continue following my Muse and keep learning about the Divine side of myself. I'm learning and creating art nearly every day and am the happiest I've ever been. I continue to meditate daily as I found it is the best practice to stay aligned to my values, to manifesting my desires, and most importantly to follow Clairity—my Muse—my Joy Seeker.

Sure, life isn't always perfect or as you have imagined it should be. For me The Weave project was a major turning point in my life. Learning to love myself; learning to forgive myself and others; learning to let go of what is out of my control, and to focus on finding out what it was I was here on this planet for my purpose. I found out that my purpose is to follow my Joy. What makes me happy, what I want my life to look like, and most importantly, what it feels like.

I grew up with so many shoulds and shouldn'ts and was in a long-term unhealthy relationship, that I found myself lost and living in the in-between for many, many years. I have no one to blame but myself and with this comes forgiveness and reconciliation like Nora did in her letter to me.

I stopped looking on the outside for love. Until I did, it was always evasive, illusive and unfulfilling. It was easy to blame others for my shortcomings, my mediocre life, and being stuck in the in-between.

The love you want, the love you desire, you already have. It's inside of you and available now.

You are my Big Why ... the reason I've written my story.

It is my hope that you will consider taking my lead, by diving deep with your inner Saboteur. Get intimate with that side of you. Get to know your Muse, your Joy seeker, the Divine, and develop all the parts by weaving them together. All of your parts make up who you were born to be.

Whole. Strong. Creative.

Remember, you can change your mind and it can change your life. When you are ready, I'm here to cheer you on!

In much love,

Darla Claire
YOUR LIFESTYLE ARCHITECT

Epilogue

I've heard them say things come in threes.

From the outside, my life appears to be pretty much perfect since I received the sacred download of The Weave. For the most part, I would agree. However, there are circumstances outside of our control that can't help but cause us to take pause and step out of our bubble of bliss.

For these reasons, I'm adding this Epilogue, as the following situations would have ended very differently for me if it weren't for the sacred process and growth I've made since then.

Siblings

Forgiveness opens the gates of Heaven.

My brother had been living on the East Coast of the country for most of his adult life. We hadn't been close, and I rarely saw him over the years. When we did see each other, our time together was always short and polite.

In 2013, I was elected by my family to travel to Connecticut to help my brother move back to Oregon to be near family.

He was in bad shape, due to his addiction to alcohol. He'd lost his job, was down in the dumps and had taken a few falls down the stairs. Fortunately for him the injuries weren't too bad, and he was on the mend. I spent several days sifting through his personal belongings, discarding what he no longer needed or wanted, and packing the rest in boxes for the move across the country. He was very little help as he was in pain, taking medication and drinking day and night. He repeatedly told me he was looking forward to coming home. I truly felt sorry for him and I knew he would be better off coming back home.

Once back in Oregon for a few weeks the family insisted he get professional help. Prior to his move, he'd promised us that he would quit drinking and get cleaned up, but he needed nudging. He eventually agreed and got the help he needed. A few months later he was clean and sober.

One day shortly after he moved into his own place and was settled in, he rang me and asked if he could come over to talk. I was hesitant but told him to come on over and I'd make him a cup of coffee. After some small talk he told me how sorry he was for treating me so badly all those years when we were growing up and occasionally as young adults. I was surprised he'd admitted abusing me, but I was very thankful and appreciative of his apology.

There were so many times I'd questioned the memories of my childhood, not knowing if they were real or if I'd just made them up in my head.

Those memories of mine were real, and he was sorry.

We reconciled; I forgave him and I finally felt I had a big brother that I loved and actually liked as a friend.

Unfortunately, he wasn't able resist the lure of the addiction and started drinking again. He passed away from alcoholism in the fall of 2017.

I had a couple of really good years with my big brother, and that I will cherish forever.

Parental Love

Over the years, I came to know that my mom did the best job she could. I know she loved me. I've come to believe most parents do the best they can with the information and skills they have at the time. Life is an evolving process, and over the years we gain knowledge and hopefully wisdom.

My mom was 19 when she had my brother. She was a baby herself. By the time she was 21 years old she was a mother of two doing her best to be a wife and homemaker. She was a perfectionist, so she had a big job on her hands.

After my parent's divorce, when I was a teenager, a few years later my mom got remarried to a kind and reliable man. Their relationship was a good one and stable.

When my mom had radical breast cancer, (in her mid 50's), she was determined to be cancer free and shortly after her treatments were finished, she started painting. She took a few art lessons, mostly using oils, and not surprising to any of us, was very talented. Painting was her creative outlet and I imagine brought her joy. She sold her paintings, co-shared a gallery with a friend and eventually was giving lessons to students.

She was a pretty amazing woman. She had a beautiful home that was always immaculate, was a fabulous cook, played the piano, designed and manufactured a lovely line of lingerie for women breast cancer survivors and she was an artist.

She was also a worrier, especially when it came to family, particularly about my brother's addiction and my unhealthy relationship with my ex-husband. She ended up getting breast cancer again in the other breast. Again, she was a survivor, a two-time survivor.

My mom was 82 years old when my brother passed. She was completely heart broken. He was her firstborn child—her true love and the air she needed to breathe.

I understood how much she loved him. Yes, it hurt a little that he was her favorite, but I understood their relationship and I loved my mom very much. She was a smart woman, and she saw my brother's flaws. Disappointed in many of his lifestyle decisions, but nonetheless, a mother's love for her child, no matter how old, never wavers.

At the time, my mom was living alone because she was no longer able to care for my stepdad who was wheelchair bound. She was completely overcome with grief. I felt so bad for her. She was inconsolable and unable to safely take care of herself as she started falling often. We moved my mom and stepdad into a beautiful new assisted care facility just a few blocks from their home. Within just a first few weeks they both seemed to adjust to their new home and happy to have the help they needed.

A couple months later, my step-dad who was almost 91 was getting weak, and had to be taken to a higher care unit.

I took my mom to see her Doctor after she'd fallen in her room, was pretty bruised and had twisted her ankle. At the end of the examination the Doctor bluntly told her if she didn't start eating more and put on some weight, she would be dead in 3 months. I saw my mom look at the Doctor in his eyes and nodded her head as if to tell him she understood and would take his advice. I was glad that she agreed to eat more to gain her strength and energy. She was healthy otherwise.

Between running my business and remodeling a home, I spent as much time with her and my stepdad as I could. My mom and I became very close, for the first time in my life I knew in my heart she loved me unconditionally, and she knew I loved her.

One month later my mom's husband, my beloved stepdad, quietly passed on April 30th while he was in the hospital. His transition was something I wasn't expecting. I'd never been with anyone that was transitioning out of this life before. The hospice caregivers were making sure he wasn't in any pain. He wasn't conscious, his breathing was labored, but I felt he knew we were there. My mom, her pastor and I were by his side; mom was being very stoic.

A woman stuck her head in the room and asked if she could come in and play her harp. At first, I was taken aback. I thought a harp? Then I told her, "Yes, that would be lovely," as I knew my mom loved harp music. The harpist situated herself at the foot of my stepdad's bed with the full-sized harp in tow. We sat there, no one was talking, we were just Being when I watched the woman watching my stepdad's labored breathing. She then placed her fingers on the strings and began playing beautiful music to the rhythm of my stepdad's breath. Strumming a string with his breathing in ... strumming with his breathing out ...

I'm not sure how long she played, but at one point I noticed my stepdad's breathing was no longer labored, and he was breathing normally. I was thinking that he was getting better and was going to recover. No one in the room was talking. The only sounds were coming from each finger strumming the cords. The rhythm of the movement of her fingers was becoming slower, and quieter. My stepdad's breathing was in complete harmony with harpist's fingers. Time seemed to stand still. Then the harpist made one last strum ... holding the string ... holding the note. At the same time, my stepdad took his last breath. As I watched his spirit leave his body and out of the room, I witnessed something holy, a time in my life I will never forget.

I watched my mom, she didn't make a sound, or shed a tear. She knew he was no longer confined by his wheelchair and was in the arms of his Lord.

This was just 7 months after my brother had passed.

Only a month and a half later my mom, 3 months to the day her Doctor told her if she didn't start eating, she would die, passed away. She couldn't go on without my brother or her husband. She didn't want to. Before she passed, we spent many hours and days together. I did my best to make sure she had all her needs met and tried to encourage her to get her strength back. I'd climb into bed with her and we'd watch girlie-girl movies together. We would just sit holding hands; often with no words between us. I knew she was getting weaker. She told me she loved me many times. I knew she did, and she knew I loved her deeply as well. Sure, we didn't always see eye to eye over the years, like most parents and their children. But the love between a mother and her child, erases all disagreements, all misunderstanding, and all that is left is an undying love.

I did have many unremarkable, insignificant days when I was growing up that I don't have clear memories of.

The gift that's often forgotten is wrapped within our unremarkable days. I know now, for my mom those days were significant, remarkable and precious to her.

This year my mom and I are taking one last trip together, on a boat trip to our last vacation spot we took together, Hawaii. Where she'll be released into the wind off the beautiful waters of the islands. It will be a remarkably significant day full of love I will remember forever.

Sacred Lessons

In a matter of months, I had three very hard events of loss in my life. I can honestly say, the Weave made these events bearable. Some would actually say I've been flourishing even more than before my family's deaths.

Because of the wealth of wisdom I received that changed who I am, I am able handle things that in the past most likely would have broken me. Instead, I didn't break. I've known many friends and family who've had significant losses and I've seen how difficult it's been for them. With the Weave in my life, I am grateful that isn't my experience. I know Clairity is by my side. I am aware of her presence often.

Fourteen miles. I'd get into my car just about every day and drive the 14 miles to see my mom. Sometimes I'd make the short drive a several times a day. It took me approximately 23 minutes to go from door to door. Those 23 minutes were my time to feel. I was feeling the loss and at times was struggling to wrap my head around it all.

I remember one early morning getting in my car and I heard the word wail. Just wail! It was Clairity and I actually believe it was also Nora. They were telling me to "wail it out," feel my feelings wholly, because if I didn't, I'd end up carrying the grief with me.

In those 14 miles, I was reminded of all I'd learned about myself since the Weave. The new tools I had been given to love myself. I know my brother, stepfather, and my mom are all well since they've crossed over. They are no longer suffering; they are with the Divine Source of love and creativity in which everyone comes from.

This is not a sad ending. It is a triumph on so many levels for me. I continue to grow and am on this fabulous journey of exploring the possibilities with this new mindset. I fully embrace that by changing my mind, I have truly changed my life!

Breathe In ... Love.

Breath Out ... Forgiveness.

Breathe In ... the Divine.

Breathe Out ... Letting Go.

"Morning Dew" for my Mom

About the Author

Darla Claire believes she's discovered the secret of how to live a fabulous life no matter what comes her way. Her world went through a major shake-up that resulted in a divine download that turned out to be an insightful, creative and fun process, teaching her to honor all parts of herself. She learned to change her negative feelings into a neutral or positive state and her thinking naturally followed. She changed her mind and it changed her life.

Darla Claire is known as the Lifestyle Architect and is Master Certified in Hypnotherapy, Timeline Therapy™, NLP Life Coaching and has wrapped it up in her signature program she calls The Weave, formerly known as the Saboteur-Muse Project. She's conducted the life-changing Saboteur-Muse Project workshops and retreats and has helped clients around the world with private sessions to transform their inner-critic into a powerful ally so they can live a life they love.

Darla continues to expand her creative adventures through her art and design. She loves spending time, known as "Nana" with her 3 awesome grandchildren. Darla and her husband, Michael currently live in Lake Oswego, Oregon with their two furry pups and 13 fish.

You can contact Darla through the websites below:

DarlaClaire.com and DarlaClaire.Art

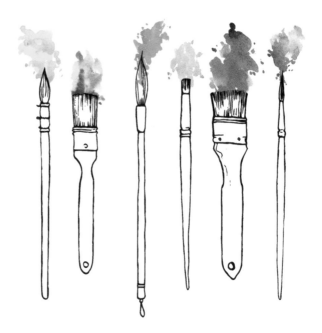

Lightning Source UK Ltd.
Milton Keynes UK
UKHW021111170322
400156UK00006B/339